SPORTS in
AMERICA
1940–1949

PHIL BARBER

SERIES FOREWORD BY LARRY KEITH

®

Facts On File, Inc.

1940–1949
Sports in America

Facts On File, Inc.
132 West 31st Street
New York NY 10001

Library of Congress Cataloging-in-Publication Data

Sports in America / produced by the Shoreline Publishing Group.
   v. cm.
Includes bibliographical references and indexes.
Contents: [1] 1910-1919 / by James Buckley, Jr. and John Walters — [2] 1920-1939 / by John Walters — [3] 1940-1949 / by Phil Barber — [4] 1950-1959 / by Jim Gigliotti — [5] 1960-1969 / by David Fischer — [6] 1970-1979 / by Timothy J. Seeberg and Jim Gigliotti — [7] 1980-1989 / by Michael Teitelbaum — [8] 1990-2003 / by Bob Woods.

ISBN 0-8160-5233-6 (hc : set : alk. paper) — ISBN 0-8160-5234-4 (hc : v. 1 : alk. paper) — ISBN 0-8160-5235-2 (hc : v. 2 : alk. paper) — ISBN 0-8160-5236-0 (hc : v. 3 : alk. paper) — ISBN 0-8160-5237-9 (hc : v. 4 : alk. paper) — ISBN 0-8160-5238-7 (hc : v. 5 : alk. paper) — ISBN 0-8160-5239-5 (hc : v. 6 : alk. paper) — ISBN 0-8160-5240-9 (hc : v. 7 :alk. paper) — ISBN 0-8160-5241-7 (hc : v. 8 : alk. paper)

1. Sports—United States—History.   I. Buckley, James, 1963-   . II. Shoreline Publishing Group. III. Facts on File, Inc.

GV583.S6826 2004
796'.0973'0904—dc22

2004004276

Produced by the Shoreline Publishing Group LLC
President/Editorial Director: James Buckley Jr.
Contributing Editors: Jim Gigliotti, Beth Adelman
Text design by Thomas Carling, Carling Design, Inc.
Cover design by Pehrsson Design and Cathy Rincon
Index by Nanette Cardon, IRIS

Photo credits: Page 1: Courtesy Sports Immortals, Inc. Jackie Robinson wore (and signed) this jersey for the Brooklyn Dodgers. In 1997, Major League Baseball retired his number 42 for all teams, honoring his pioneering 1947 season (see page 66). All interior photos courtesy AP/Wide World except for the following: Corbis: 8, 26, 27, 34, 47, 49, 68; NFL Photos: 57, 82. Sports icons by Bob Eckstein.

Printed in the United States of America.

VH PKG 10 9 8 7 6 5 4 3 2 1

This book is printed on acid-free paper.

CONTENTS

Jackie Robinson, baseball player and barrier breaker (page 66)

FOREWORD

BY LARRY KEITH

IN THE FALL OF 1984, STUDENTS AT COLUMBIA University's prestigious Graduate School of Journalism requested that a new course be added to the curriculum—sports journalism.

Sports journalism? In the graduate program of an Ivy League institution? Get serious.

But the students were serious, and, as students will do, they persisted. Eventually, the school formed a committee to interview candidates for the position of "adjunct professor." As it happened, though, the committee wasn't just looking for a professional sports journalist to teach the course part time. That august body wanted to hear clear and convincing arguments that the course should be offered at all.

In other words, did sports matter? And, more to the point, should an institution that administered the Pulitzer Prize, the highest award in journalism, associate itself with the coverage of "fun and games?"

Two decades later, I am pleased to say that Columbia did decide to offer the course and that it remains in the curriculum. With modest pride, I confess that I helped make the arguments that swayed the committee and became the new adjunct professor.

I reflected on that experience when the *Sports in America* editors invited me to write the Foreword to this important series. I said then, and I say now, "Sport is an integral part of American society and requires the attention of a competent and vigilant press." For our purposes here, I might also add, "because it offers insights to our history and culture."

Sports in America is much more than a compilation of names, dates, and facts. Each volume chronicles accomplishments, advances, and expansions of the possible. Not just in the physical ability to run faster, jump higher, or hit a ball farther, but in the cognitive ability to create goals and analyze how to achieve them. In this way, sports, the sweaty offspring of recreation and competition, resemble any other field of endeavor. I certainly wouldn't equate the race for a gold medal with the race to the moon, but the essentials are the same: the application of talent, determination, research, practice, and hard work to a meaningful objective.

Sports matter because they represent the best and worst of us. They give us flesh-and-blood examples of courage and skill. They often embody a heroic human interest story, about overcoming poverty, injustice, injury, or disease. The phrase, "Sports is a microcosm of life," could also be, "Life is a microcosm of sports." Consider racial issues, for example. When Jackie Robinson of the Brooklyn Dodgers broke through Major League Baseball's color barrier in 1947, the significance extended beyond the national pastime. Precisely because baseball *was* the national pastime, this important event reverberated throughout American society.

To be sure, black stars from individual sports had preceded him (notably Joe Louis in boxing and Jesse Owens in track and field), and others would follow (Arthur Ashe in tennis and Tiger Woods in golf), but Robinson stood out as an important member of a *team*. He wasn't just playing with the Dodgers, he was traveling with them, dressing with them, eating with them, living with them. The benefits of integration, the recognition of its humanity, could be appreciated far beyond the borough of Brooklyn.

Sports have always been a laboratory for social issues. Robinson integrated big-league box scores eight years before the U.S. Supreme Court ordered the integration of public schools. Women's official debut in the Olympic Games, though limited to swimming, came in 1912, seven years before they got the right to vote. So even if these sports were late in opening their doors, in another way they were ahead of their time. And if it was necessary to break down some of those doors—Title IX support since 1972 for female college athletics comes to mind—so be it.

Another area of social importance, particularly as it affects young people, is substance abuse. High school, college, and professional teams are united in their opposition to the illegal use of drugs, tobacco, and alcohol. In most venues, testing is mandatory and tolerance is zero. Perhaps the most celebrated case occurred at the 1988 Olympic Games, when Canada's Ben Johnson surrendered his 100-meter gold medal after failing a drug test. Some athletes have lost their careers, and even their lives, to substance abuse. Other athletes have used their fame and success to caution young people about submitting to peer pressure and making poor choices.

Fans care about sports and sports personalities because they provide entertainment and identity. But they aren't the only ones who root, root, root for the home team. Government bodies come on board because sports spur local economies. When a city council votes to help underwrite the cost of a stadium or give financial advantages to the owners of a team, it affects the pocketbook of every taxpayer, not to mention the local ecosystem. When high schools and colleges allocate significant resources to athletics, administrators believe they are serving the greater good, but at what cost? These decisions are relevant far beyond the sports page.

In World War II, America's sporting passion inspired President Franklin Roosevelt to say professional games should not be cancelled. He felt the benefits to the national psyche outweighed the security risk of gathering huge crowds at central locations. In 2001, another generation of fans also continued to attend large-scale sports events because to do otherwise would "let the terrorists win." Being there, yelling your lungs out, cheering victory and bemoaning defeat, is a cleansing, even therapeutic exercise. The security check at the gate is just another price of stepping inside.

Unfortunately, there's a downside to all this. The notion that "Sports build character" is better expressed "Sports *reveal* character." We've witnessed too many coaches and athletes break the rules of fair play and good conduct, on and off the field. We've even seen violence and cheating in youth sports, often by parents of a (supposed) future superstar. We've watched fans "celebrate" championships with destructive behavior. I would argue, however, that these flaws are the exception, not the rule, that the good of sports outweighs the bad, that many of life's success stories took root on an athletic field.

Any serious examination of sports leads, inevitably, to the question of athletes as role models. Pro basketball star Charles Barkley created quite a stir in 1993 when he declared in a Nike shoe commercial, "I am not paid to be a role model." The knee-jerk response was, "But kids look up to you!" Barkley was right to raise the issue, though. He was saying that, in making lifestyle choices in language, clothing, and behavior, young people should look elsewhere for role models—ideally in their own home, to responsible parents.

The fact remains, however, that athletes occupy an exalted place in our society, at least when they are magnified in the mass media, and especially in the big-business, money-motivated sports. The athletes we venerate can be as young as a high school basketball player or as old as a Hall of Famer. (They can even be dead, as Babe Ruth's commercial longevity attests.) They are honored and coddled in a way few mortals are. We are quick—too quick—to excuse their excesses and ignore their indulgences. They influence the way we live (the food on our table, the cars in our driveway) and think (Ted Williams inspired patriotism as a fighter pilot during World War II and the Korean conflict; Muhammad Ali's opposition to the Vietnam War on religious grounds, validated by the Supreme Court, inspired the peace movement). No wonder we elect them—track stars, football coaches, baseball pitchers—to represent us in government. Meanwhile, television networks pay exorbitant sums to sports leagues so their teams can pay fortunes for players' services.

It has always been this way. If we, as a nation, love sports, then we, quite naturally, will love the men and women who play them best. In return, they give us entertainment, release, and inspiration. From the beginning of the 20th century until now, *Sports in America* is their story—and ours.

Larry Keith is a former writer and editor at Sports Illustrated. *He covered baseball and college basketball and edited the official Olympic programs in 1996, 2000 and 2002. He is a former adjunct professor of sports journalism at Columbia University and is a member of the Board of Visitors of the University of North Carolina School of Journalism.*

INTRODUCTION
1940–1949

WE OFTEN TALK ABOUT THE WAYS sports and society mix, the way they affect and shape one another. The distinction blurred almost completely in the 1940s, when the forces of change and conflict intruded mightily upon the games people played.

As the decade dawned, World War II gripped much of the world. By 1940, the United States was a behind-the-scenes participant, sending arms and equipment to allies that included Great Britain. But as the Axis powers—Germany, Japan, and Italy—gobbled up territory, it appeared inevitable that America would join the fight outright. The decision was cemented on December 7, 1941, when the Japanese bombed the U.S. Navy fleet at Pearl Harbor in Hawaii.

Soon many of America's best young men and women, and most of its natural resources, were headed for war.

The Selective Service Act was passed in the fall of 1940, making it possible for the government to draft men into the armed forces, and within two years at least 31 million men had registered for the draft. More than half of them wound up serving, and inevitably, some were drawn from the sports world. Stars and nobodies, veterans and rookies, all of them mobilized. The National Football League (NFL) lost 638 of its players, coaches, and officials to the armed forces; 66 of them were decorated in battle and 21 died in combat, including 12 active players.

The casualties certainly weren't limited to the big team sports. Torger Tokle, a Norwegian immigrant who set an American ski jump record in 1941, then broke it twice more (topping out at 289 feet), died while fighting in the Italian mountains with a U.S. ski-patrol force in 1944.

Even the athletes who stayed in the United States made sacrifices. Sports equipment manufacturers set a tone for the era by urging their consumers to "use it up, wear it out, make do, or do without." With rubber in short supply, most tennis and golf balls manufactured during World

Day of Infamy *December 7, 1941: The* USS Arizona *blows up in Pearl Harbor during the Japanese attack.*

War II were made of a combination of reclaimed and crude rubber, or a synthetic alternative. Tennis players called the mushy balls they played with "victory balls." Golfers complained that an average drive of 225 yards shrunk to 210 with their new balls.

Along the way, some now-revered traditions were conceived. In baseball, for example, crowds started singing the National Anthem before every game, and they kept the tradition going even after the war ended. Major League Baseball also began to play more night games during the war, in part to accommodate factory workers. The Westinghouse Electric Co. supported the idea by reporting that stadium lights would use less power than the desk lamps of individual fans reading at home.

1940-1949

The Japanese, huge baseball fans themselves, knew how important sports were to Americans. They tried to jam broadcasts of the World Series over the Armed Forces Radio Network, and U.S. soldiers reported their Japanese enemies shouted, "To hell with Babe Ruth!" as they stormed fortified positions.

Finally, in 1945, after nearly four years of intense fighting, World War II came to an end. Americans celebrated by flocking to ballparks, stadiums, courts, and rinks. Life returned to normal. "Dreams of baseball were dreams of sanity," Arthur Daley wrote in *The New York Times* on April 14, 1946. "To the dreamers the game was a symbol of the things-that-were, of the things-yet-to-be."

America entered World War II in the throes of an economic depression. Now the economy was humming, ramped up by the war effort, and sports fans had money to spend. The 1945 World Series, played just one month after the Japanese surrendered, set records for attendance (333,457 people) and gate receipts (nearly $1.6 million). In 1946, the Indianapolis Speedway welcomed 175,000 people to the Indy 500 auto race, and basketball crowds at all professional and college levels totaled some 75 million. Clearly, Americans were ready for some recreation.

But sports, like other segments of American culture, did not return to business as usual after the war. The government had asked its populace to display a sense of teamwork during the conflict, and many now demanded that the concept be applied more broadly in peacetime. Specifically, African-Americans were demanding equality, and many whites were ready to back them up. As baseball commissioner Albert "Happy" Chandler said, "If they [blacks] can fight and die on Okinawa, Guadalcanal, in the South Pacific, they can play ball in America."

In 1946, two football teams in competing leagues—the National Football League's Los Angeles Rams and the All-America Football Conference's Cleveland Browns—suited up African-American players. It was a relatively quiet achievement for the Rams' Kenny Washington and Woody Strode and the Browns' Bill Willis and Marion Motley.

By contrast, when Jackie Robinson joined baseball's Brooklyn Dodgers a

Other Kinds of Uniforms *Yankees superstar Joe DiMaggio (left) and Dodgers sparkplug Pee Wee Reese (second from right) were among many athletes who joined the armed forces during the war.*

year later, it was one of the biggest sports stories of the decade, or, some might say, of the century. Baseball was by far the most popular sport in the 1940s, and its color barrier had been silently enforced since the turn of the century. But Dodgers president Branch Rickey decided the time had come to shatter that barrier, and he chose Robinson to do it. The 1947 season tested Robinson's resolve, but by October he helped Brooklyn get to the World Series and was voted Rookie of the Year for both leagues. The game never looked back. The Cleveland Indians' Larry Doby integrated the American League in 1948, and many other teams soon followed suit.

If the 1940s brought growing pains to some of the established professional sports, they announced the birth of others. The National Basketball Association, NASCAR, the Ladies Professional Golf Association, and a legitimate professional tennis tour all arose in the second half of the decade.

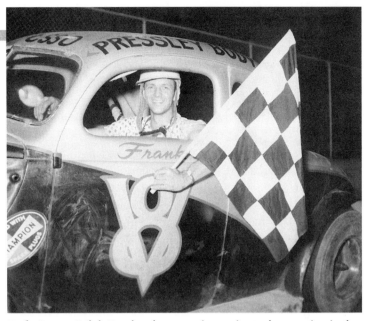

Early Days *Ralph Earnhardt was a pioneer in stock car racing in the 1940s and was one of NASCAR's first top drivers. Ralph was also the father of seven-time NASCAR champion Dale Earnhardt and the grandfather of today's popular young driver Dale Earnhardt, Jr.*

Having survived the crucible of war and having begun to fight the battle for integration, American sports were ready for a golden age.

1940

Brotherhood Canceled

The year 1940 was supposed to have been a time of national pride for Japan. The emerging country was scheduled to host both the Winter Olympics in Sapporo and the Summer Olympics in Tokyo.

By 1937, that plan had come undone. In 1931, the Japanese government invaded Manchuria, the northeastern peninsula of China. Japan attacked into the heart of China in 1937, beginning a war that would last seven years, spread throughout the Pacific, and be the scene of countless acts of atrocity. Mired in conflict, Japan canceled its Olympics.

As alternatives, the International Olympic Committee (IOC) selected St. Moritz, Switzerland, for the Winter Games and Helsinki, Finland, for the Summer Games. However, Switzerland—one of the few European nations that would not be drawn into the coming war—and the IOC then became embroiled in a dispute. The Swiss insisted that ski instructors should not be considered professionals, and thus should be allowed to compete in the Games, which were amateur-only. The IOC refused, and withdrew its offer.

The committee then turned to Garmisch-Partenkirchen, Germany (which had hosted the 1936 Winter Games). But that plan fell through, too. After signing a non-aggression pact with the Soviet Union, the Germans invaded Poland in 1939. Britain and France immediately declared war—the opening salvo of World War II. The Soviets, meanwhile, occupied Finland in November 1939.

By 1940, the Nazis were sweeping through Belgium and the Netherlands, and London was under heavy bombardment. The United States was supplying money and material to Britain and its allies, but it was only a matter of time before America's role became more active. Clearly, this was no time for international sporting events. The IOC canceled the Games for the first time in the modern era.

The 1944 Olympic Games, scheduled for London and Cortina d'Ampezzo, Italy, would be canceled as well.

The Flying Dutchman

Among the world's pole vaulters, the height of 15 feet had become something of a barrier. Many tried to top it, but none could. Finally, on April 13,

Record Setter *Before the fiberglass pole was developed, Cornelius Warmerdam soared 15 feet using a wood pole.*

Cornelius "Dutch" Warmerdam cleared that elusive height. Warmerdam, a 24-year-old high school teacher, was competing for the San Francisco Olympic Club at Berkeley, California.

Warmerdam's record-breaking vault measured 15 feet, 1 1/8 inches. This was no lucky leap. Competing at Fresno, California, on June 29, he bettered the mark by nearly two inches. And he continued to

1940

shatter his own record, inch by inch, until he hit 15 feet, 8 1/2 inches in 1943. He retired from the sport in 1944, having topped 15 feet an incredible 43 times.

Observers of the day swear no one has ever exhibited better form in the pole vault than Warmerdam. His vaults are far lower than those today, but Dutch made his vaults with a wooden pole. The modern fiberglass pole didn't come along until the 1960s, and soon after, men were vaulting more than 17 feet.

One Tough Feller

The Cleveland Indians' hard-throwing pitcher, Bob Feller (b.1918), had been the class of the American League in 1939, leading the league in wins (24), innings pitched (296), and strikeouts (246). So everyone expected him to have a big season in 1940. They just didn't know how quickly he'd get rolling. Feller took the mound on April 16 and threw a no-hitter, blanking the Chicago White Sox 1–0. It is still the only Opening Day no-hitter in Major League Baseball history.

The 21-year-old Feller had an exceptional season. He won 27 games for the Indians, with 261 strikeouts in 320 innings and a league-leading earned run average (ERA) of 2.61. (ERA is a key measure of a pitcher's success; it shows how many earned runs a pitcher allows every nine innings.)

Yankees Go Home

The New York Yankees had another dynasty going in the late 1930s. They won four consecutive World Series from 1936 through 1939, and they didn't lose a game in the 1938 and 1939 Series. Outfielder Joe DiMaggio (1914–1999) again paced the team in 1940, leading the American League with a .352 batting average (the total number of base hits divided by the number of times a player has been at bat) and 133 runs batted in (RBI, the number of runs scored as a result of the player's at-bats).

This time, however, the Bronx Bombers fell short. In a tight three-team race, it was the Detroit Tigers who beat the Cleveland Indians (by a game) and the Yankees (by two games) to take the pennant. The Tigers were powered by a couple of mighty sluggers: outfielder Hank Greenberg (1911–1986; a .340 batting average and a league-leading 41 home runs in 1940) and first baseman Rudy York (33 homers and 134 RBI). Their best pitcher, Bobo Newsom, won 21 games and lost only five.

Pitching ruled the National League in 1940, and no team had better arms than the Cincinnati Reds. Bucky Walters led the league in wins (22) and innings pitched (305), and had a dazzling ERA of 2.48. Paul Derringer, meanwhile, won 20 games. Together they had 55 complete games and pitched 602 innings. The Reds were only average at the plate, but they had brilliant fielders to back up the pitchers.

The World Series in October went seven games, and was largely a contest between Walters and Newsom. Both were nearly invincible. Walters won two complete games, giving up only eight hits and three runs. His catcher was Jimmy Wilson, a 40-year-old coach who was filling in for Ernie Lombardi, who got hurt in game wo. Newsom won the first and fifth games, even though his father died after watching the victorious game one. Newsom valiantly pitched game seven on just one day of rest, and lost to Derringer as the Reds claimed their first championship in 21 years on October 8. For the Series, though, Newsom gave up a mere four runs in 26 innings.

Undaunted by his personal losses, the colorful Newsom arrived at spring training the following season in a car with a neon sign that read "Bobo" and a horn that played the popular song "Hold That Tiger."

Chicago Punts Football

The University of Chicago football team had plenty of success on the field. The school had, in fact, produced the nation's first Heisman Trophy winner, Jay Berwanger, in 1935. But in 1940, University President Robert Hutchins shocked the student body by announcing that the school was dropping its football program. "There is no doubt that football has been a major handicap to education in the United States," Hutchins said in an address. He noted with scorn that 50 percent of Big Ten football players were physical-education majors.

The president wrapped up his argument by stating, "I think it is a good thing for this country to have one important university discontinue football."

If Hutchins hoped for other colleges to follow suit, he was disappointed. But the University of Chicago still has no football team—preferring, instead, to churn out Nobel Prize winners.

T Time for Frankie

Few college football teams were more inept than the Stanford University Indians in 1939. The Indians finished 1–7–1, losing every Pacific Coast Conference game they played. But in 1940,

Suited to the T *Stanford quarterback Frankie Albert's success with the T formation helped make it the standard for football teams.*

The Beginning of the End

Before 1935, NFL teams passed the ball only out of desperation, or as a form of trickery. Don Hutson (1913–1997) helped change that—not by throwing the ball, but by catching it better than anyone had before.

They called Hutson the Alabama Antelope. He was fast, with reliable hands and great moves. One of his favorite moves involved grabbing a goal post (the posts were on the goal line in those days) with one arm and spinning himself away from a defender.

During his 11-year career (1935–1945) with Green Bay, Hutson led the NFL in receiving eight times. In 1942

he caught 74 passes; the next highest total was a distant 27. In 1944 he scored 29 points on four touchdowns while also kicking five extra points (after touchdowns) in a single quarter. He retired with 99 touchdowns—an NFL record that stood for 44 years.

Hutson became the first receiver to regularly see double coverage (where two defenders cover a single offensive player). And even that usually wasn't enough. "I just concede him two touchdowns a game and hope we can score more," Chicago Bears owner George Halas (1895–1983) said.

Stanford benefited from the decision at Chicago (see page 13) and hired that university's former coach, the innovative Clark Shaughnessy. The coach had developed a T-formation offensive scheme, which sent men in motion before the ball was snapped and used many more passing plays than other formations, and it was about to take the football world by storm.

Stanford began the season in September against a pretty good University of San Francisco team and won easily, 27–0. The Indians proceeded to notch victories against the University of Oregon (13–0), the University of Santa Clara (7–6), and Washington State University (26–14). Still, few thought Stanford could beat the University of Southern California (USC) on October 26. USC hadn't lost a game since 1938 and had beaten Stanford three times in a row.

With three minutes to go, the game was tied 7–7. Then, quarterback Frankie Albert started faking handoffs and turn-

ing them into play-action passes (passe made after pretending to hand off th ball). This was the strength of the T, and n one had ever handled the ball better tha Albert. He drove the Indians 80 yards fc the go-ahead touchdown, then intercept ed a USC pass with a little over a minut left and returned it for another scor Stanford won 21–7.

Powered by Albert, fullback Norr Standlee, and slashing halfback Pet Kmetovic, the Indians finished the regu lar season 10–0 and wrapped up a magi cal season by defeating the University c Nebraska 21–13 in the Rose Bowl o January 1. Within five years, most footba teams in America—at every level of play— were using the T formation.

The Prime of Old 98

At the turn of the decade, few ath letes could bring a crowd to its fee like Tommy Harmon (1919–1990), th University of Michigan's do-everythin football halfback. "Old 98"—a reference to Harmon's jersey number—played offense and defense for the Wolverines. He was a productive passer and a sensational open-field runner who shredded defenses in 1939 and 1940, winning the Heisman Trophy as a senior. He was at his best against the University of California at Berkeley (known as Cal) in 1940, scoring on sensational runs of 94, 72, 86, and 80 yards. He scored three touchdowns and passed for another in the Wolverines' 40–0 rout of rival Ohio State later in the season.

After college, Harmon signed with the New York Americans of the American Football League, a short-lived rival to the NFL. He later played two seasons (1946–47) for the Los Angeles Rams. But that was after a stint as an Air Corps fighter pilot in World War II that would leave him with a Silver Star, a Purple Heart, and an injured leg. He just wouldn't be the runner who had thrilled fans at the collegiate level.

Asked to compare some of the great backs he had seen over his long and decorated career, famed coach Amos Alonzo Stagg (1862–1965) once said, "I'll take Harmon on my team, and you can have the rest."

Chasing a Bulldog

Clyde "Bulldog" Turner was a heck of a football player, but not many people had the opportunity to watch him play at tiny Hardin-Simmons College in Abilene, Texas. One person who did see Turner happened to be a friend of George Richards, owner of the NFL's Detroit Lions. The friend was so impressed with Turner during a game against Loyola College of Los Angeles that he called Richards at his Los Angeles home and told him, "Get down here."

Richards arrived for the second half of the game and was equally impressed. He paid the center to tell other NFL teams he wasn't interested in pro football. But on draft day, Lions coach Gus Henderson, figuring Turner was already secured for his team, drafted University of Southern California quarterback Doyle Nave in the first round. The Chicago Bears then drafted Turner.

Richards was furious. He fired Henderson and tried to get Turner to quit football for a year. The league found out and fined Richards $5,000 for tampering. He then sold the Lions to Fred Mandel. Bulldog Turner, meanwhile, played 13 years in Chicago and wound up in the Pro Football Hall of Fame.

73–0!

The NFL's fiercest rivalry of the era pitted the Chicago Bears against the Washington Redskins. They played for the league championship in 1937, and again in 1942 and 1943. Each team had a great passer, Washington's Sammy Baugh (b. 1914) and Chicago's Sid Luckman (1916–1998). Most important, the two team owners—George Halas of the Bears and George Preston Marshall of the Redskins—were proud and fiery men who basically couldn't stand one another.

After Washington edged Chicago 7–3 on November 17, Halas and his players angrily complained about a controversial call made in the final seconds. Marshall

1940

responded by labeling the Bears "a bunch of crybabies."

With the Redskins winning the Eastern Division on the strength of a 9–2 record and the Bears capturing the Western Division at 8–3, the stage was set for a rematch. Halas, the head coach as well as the owner, fumed about Marshall's remark as the game approached. He also recruited Stanford University coach Clark Shaughnessy (see page 14), who tinkered with the offense in the days leading up to the grudge match on December 8.

The Redskins didn't know what hit them. Fifty-five seconds into the game, Bears fullback Bill Osmanski took a handoff and blazed down the left sideline. End George Wilson blasted two defenders out of the way, and Osmanski was gone for a 68-yard touchdown. The next time they got the ball, Luckman drove the Bears 80 yards and scored on a quarterback sneak. On the first play of the next possession, fullback Joe Maniaci raced 42 yards for a touchdown. It was 21–0 at the end of the first quarter, 28–0 at halftime, and it only got worse in the second half.

This was the first pro football game to be broadcast over an entire radio network—120 stations via the Mutual Broadcasting System, which paid $2,500 for the rights—and the announcer, the legendary Red Barber (1908–1992), couldn't believe what he was seeing. "The touchdowns came so quickly there for awhile, I felt like I was the cashier at a grocery store," Barber said. "It is a very good thing I went over the roster of the Bears. I believe I wound up having to say every player's name on the list. In fact, I believe they all scored touchdowns."

Indeed, 10 different Bears took the ball into the end zone. And Luckman didn't even play in the second half. Halas pulled many of his starters as the margin grew. When the score reached 67–0, the public address announcer at Griffith Stadium bravely reminded Redskins fans that it was never too early to order tickets for 1941. He was drowned out by boos.

By late in the game, footballs were scarce because so many extra-point kicks had landed in the stands. So the officials ordered the Bears to run or pass for their conversions. They missed four extra points in all, detracting only a bit from the dizzying final score of 73–0. The NFL has never had a bigger blowout, before or since.

Justice on the Field

The NFL's leading rusher in 1940 was a man who would gain more acclaim in a black robe than he ever did in a football jersey. He was Byron "Whizzer" White (b.1917), who went on to a 31-year tenure as a U.S. Supreme Court Justice, after being appointed by President John F. Kennedy in 1962.

White, a celebrated student-athlete at the University of Colorado, first led the professional league's rushers as a rookie with the Pittsburgh Pirates in 1938. He then spent a year at Oxford University in Britain, studying on a Rhodes scholarship. He returned to play for the Detroit Lions in 1940 and used his shifty moves to gain 514 yards on the ground. After one more season, he left football and turned his attention to larger matters. His rise to legal fame didn't surprise any of his teammates.

As Lions coach George Clark once said, "While the other guys were playing cards for five cents a point, White would get out his glasses, his pipe, and his law books and start studying."

Other Milestones of 1940

✔ On February 28, WXBS (later WNBC) televised the first college basketball games. The ground-breaking broadcast was a double-header: University of Pittsburgh vs. Fordham University and New York University vs. Georgetown, at New York's Madison Square Garden.

✔ The University of Illinois won the first intercollegiate gymnastics team championship on May 11.

✔ Basketball's Harlem Globetrotters defeated the Chicago Bruins to claim something called the World Championship Tournament. The Bruins were owned by George

Ronald Reagan as Gipp

Halas, who also ran the NFL's Chicago Bears.

✔ Belle Martel of Van Nuys, California, became the first female boxing referee when she presided over eight fights in San Bernardino.

✔ The movie *Knute Rockne, All-American* made its debut. Future President Ronald Reagan starred as George Gipp.

✔ Harry Reeves, a lieutenant in the Detroit police department, won the first of six national pistol shooting championships. The six titles came over a 15-year period.

In all, Chicago rushed for 381 yards, completed 7 of 10 passes for another 138 yards and intercepted eight passes. Washington replaced Baugh with Frank Filchock, but it hardly mattered. As Bears tackle George Musso said, "It was the perfect football game. You can't play better than we did that day."

Marshall was predictably upset after the game. He told reporters his defense looked like "a roomful of maidens [young women] going after a mouse," and his offense wasn't much better.

It was a dark day in the nation's capital, where politicians and generals already worried about the German bombing of London and the occupation of Paris. But in Chicago, for one day at least, there was pure joy.

1941

Whirlaway Crowned

On May 3, jockey Eddie Arcaro (1916–1997) rode the horse Whirlaway to a record time of 2:01 2/5 in the Kentucky Derby. A week later the duo claimed the Preakness Stakes. The Belmont Stakes was nearly a month later, on June 7, and more than 30,000 racing fans turned out to see whether Arcaro and Whirlaway could win racing's coveted Triple Crown.

Whirlaway was a spirited chestnut colt, the son of Blenheim II and Dustwhirl. He was bred on Calumet Farms, the country's premier Thoroughbred breeder. Calumet's owner, Warren Wright, missed the Belmont to attend his son's graduation ceremony, but insiders figured his absence was because he just wasn't worried about the race. His horse, after all, was a heavy 1-to-4 favorite.

Arcaro's usual strategy aboard the tireless Whirlaway was to hang back until the final stretch. "But at the mile post, there was no pace," he explained later. "It was very slow. So I yelled to those other jocks, 'I'm leaving.'"

And so he was. Whirlaway bolted to the front of the pack before the half-mile mark (the race was a mile and a half) and won by three lengths, making Whirlaway the fifth horse to capture the Triple Crown. Arcaro never had to use the whip in this one.

Conn's Folly

Joe Louis was making a mockery of boxing's heavyweight division, defeating all challengers and making it look easy. When former light-heavyweight champion Billy Conn, a tough Irish-American from Pittsburgh, moved up to take a shot at Louis, nobody gave him much of a

On the Way to 56 *With this swing, Joe DiMaggio advanced his hitting streak to 39 consecutive games (page 20).*

chance. In fact, the only person who seemed to take Conn seriously was Conn himself. "He won't get away from me when he's hurt," the brash 25-year-old told reporters, referring to Louis.

The two boxers met at the Polo Grounds in Manhattan on June 18. Promoters set up wooden chairs on the New York Giants' baseball field, and the 54,487 in attendance included many uniformed soldiers and sailors. Just about everyone expected Conn, who was 25 pounds lighter, to dance away from Louis in an at-tempt to tire him out. But he charged right at the champion and shocked the crowd with his effectiveness. It was an action-packed fight. Conn was cut on the bridge of his nose and over his right eye in the fifth round, while Louis got a bloody nose in the ninth round.

By the 12th round, it was clear that Conn had out-boxed Louis. Most observers agreed that all he had to do was avoid the big man's right cross for three more rounds, and Conn would be the new heavyweight champion.

Conn on the Canvas *Joe Louis heads for a neutral corner while the referee moves in for the count after Louis decked challenger Billy Conn in their June heavyweight fight, which Conn almost won.*

56 for 56

On May 15, Joe DiMaggio got a single in four at-bats against the Chicago White Sox. No surprise there. New York Yankees fans were used to seeing DiMaggio on base. The centerfielder got hits in his next game, and the next, and the game after, and before long he was building an impressive hitting streak.

DiMaggio stretched it to 20 straight games on June 3 (a single against the Detroit Tigers) and to 25 games on June 10 (a single against the Chicago White Sox). Soon the entire nation was checking his performance in the morning papers and getting radio bulletins on every at-bat. Fans flocked to his games. Official scorers admitted to feeling the pressure (they didn't want to end or prolong the streak on a questionable play), but the unflappable DiMaggio never changed expression.

On June 28 he got a single and a double against the Philadelphia A's, tying George Sisler's (1893–1973) major-league mark of 41 consecutive games with a hit. DiMaggio broke the record the next day, singling against the Washington Senators. He made it to 50 games on July 11, pounding a home run and three singles against the St. Louis Browns.

It all came to an end on July 17, before 67,468 people in Cleveland (to that point, the largest crowd ever to see a night baseball game), but Joltin' Joe DiMaggio didn't go quietly. In two of his first three at-bats against Indians pitcher Al Smith, he ripped the ball down the third base line. Each time, the Indians' Ken Keltner made a superb stop and threw across the field for the out.

Louis knew it, too, so he came out swinging in the 13th round. Instead of covering up and moving away, Conn decided to trade punches with the champion. It was a brave but foolhardy tactic.

Louis stunned Conn with a thunderous right to the jaw, then launched a left-right combination that knocked the challenger flat. The referee counted out Conn with only two seconds left in the round, and Louis remained heavyweight champion.

After the fight, the two boxers were mutually respectful. "Joe, you should've let me win that fight. Think of all the money we could make on the return," Conn said with a smile.

"I loaned you my title for 12 rounds," Louis replied, "and you couldn't keep it."

Smith walked DiMaggio in his second at-bat. When DiMaggio came to bat in the eighth inning, righthanded knuckleball pitcher Jim Bagby was on the mound and the bases were loaded. The crowd was on pins and needles. The Yankees star hit a bouncing ball to deep shortstop, where Cleveland player-manager Lou Boudreau turned it into a double play.

DiMaggio nearly got another chance. The Indians went into the bottom of the ninth trailing 4–1. But they scored twice and placed a man on third base with no outs. Had they gotten him home, DiMaggio was due to bat in the 10th inning. But base-running blunders sealed a 4–3 New York victory, and the end of the hitting streak at 56 games.

Even after the 0-for-3 day in Cleveland, baseball fans weren't ready to forget the run. Within weeks, a song called "Joltin' Joe DiMaggio" (performed by Les Brown and his Orchestra, with Betty Bonney on vocals) hit number 12 on the pop charts. Today, many still refer to the streak as the game's "unbeatable record." Right or wrong, it hasn't been beaten yet.

The Hitting Machine

During his sensational 56-game hitting streak, Joe DiMaggio batted for a robust .408 average. During that same span, the Boston Red Sox's Ted Williams (1918–2002) actually outdid Joltin' Joe, hitting .410. When DiMaggio's streak ended, fans across the nation swiftly took notice of Williams.

No American Leaguer had hit .400 since 1923, when Harry Heilmann of the Detroit Tigers led the league at .403. Now

Mr. Triple Crown

Jockey Eddie Arcaro was known as "The Master," and it wasn't just because he won so often—although winning was certainly part of the legacy. (He won 4,779 races in his career, including five times in the Kentucky Derby, six in the Belmont Stakes, and six in the Preakness Stakes.) What truly defined Arcaro were his quiet confidence in the saddle and his laborious devotion to his profession.

George Edward Arcaro was born in Cincinnati, Ohio, in 1916. By the time he retired from racing in 1962, *Sports Illustrated* called him "the most famous man to ride a horse since Paul Revere." He won the Triple Crown atop Whirlaway in 1941 (see page 18) and again with Citation in 1948, and he barely missed with Nashua in 1955, finishing a close second in the Derby. Arcaro had an uncanny knack for avoiding bad position on the track, and he was one of the first jockeys to switch the whip from hand to hand.

After retiring, he continued to have an impact on the sport. Arcaro was founder and first president of the Jockeys Guild, which provided health insurance and other employment benefits to the long-overlooked riders.

Joltin' Joe

Someone once asked Joe DiMaggio why he played so hard day in and day out. He replied, "There might be someone in the park who's never seen me play before."

Or there might not be. Between 1936 and 1951, sports fans of all stripes (and especially pinstripes) filled ballparks to see the man they called the Yankee Clipper.

DiMaggio couldn't hit the ball as far as his Yankees' predecessor, Babe Ruth (1895–1948), or the slugger who followed him to Yankees' fame, Mickey Mantle (1931–1995). But he could do it all. He hit home runs (361), he hit for average (.325), and he ranged around center field like a gazelle. With his long stride and fluid grace, he made it all look easy. And while his reserved, private nature might today be viewed as aloofness, in the 1940s DiMaggio was considered the epitome of class. It didn't hurt that he played for the dominant team of the era, in the country's biggest media market.

Raised in San Francisco, the son of a fisherman, DiMaggio preceded two brothers—Vince and Dom—in the big leagues. Dom was a noted player in his own right. But it was Joe who inspired songs and poems and married America's biggest movie star, Marilyn Monroe, in 1954. And it's Joe who has come to symbolize the beauty and grace of sports in a purer time.

Williams was making a serious run at the mark. As August turned to September, his average stood at .413. Then he went cold.

On the last day of the season, September 28, with a doubleheader to play, Williams was batting .39955. His manager, Joe Cronin (1906–1984), who was doubly busy hitting .311 as the Red Sox's shortstop, knew that the league would round up Williams' average to an even .400. With Boston far behind the Yankees in the standings, Cronin suggested the slugger take the day off and preserve his mark. Williams refused.

In the first game of the doubleheader he had four hits, including a home run. He got two more hits in the second game. All in all, he went six for eight and raised his average to a sparkling .406.

The average was only part of a phenomenal season for Williams. He led the league with 37 home runs, 145 walks, and 135 runs scored. And perhaps most impressive, he struck out only 27 times. It has been more than 60 years since Williams hit .400. No one has done it since.

The Winner Wore a Corset

The 1941 U.S. Open golf tournament was held in June at Fort Worth, Texas, in the home state of some of the sport's top competitors, including Jimmy Demaret, Ben Hogan (1912–1997), and Byron Nelson (b.1912). Fans gathered at the Colonial Club to cheer their local heroes, and the weather was pure Texas. When the tournament began, the fairways were soaked with rain; when it ended, the thermometer read 95 degrees.

The winner was unexpected. Craig Wood, 46 years old, had such chronic back pain that he was forced to wear a corset while playing. But he shot a 284, outlasting Denny Shute at 287. The resilient Wood also captured the Masters in 1941.

Go Go Gophers

The Big Ten Conference was the seat of power in college football before World War II. And from 1933 through 1941, the dominant Big Ten team was Bernie Bierman's University of Minnesota Gophers. Minnesota's apex came in 1940 and 1941, when the team went undefeated over the course of the two seasons (16–0) and claimed back-to-back national championships.

Not that the victories always came easily. In 1940 Minnesota had narrowly beaten star halfback Tommy Harmon and the University of Michigan, winning 7–6. In 1941 the Gophers trailed Northwestern University 7–2 and seemed headed for defeat. But they called a play without a signal, caught Northwestern sleeping, and scored on a long touchdown run by Brad Higgins.

Halfback Bruce Smith, the pride of the 1941 Minnesota squad, won the Heisman Trophy.

The NFL's New Horseman

Since its start in 1920, the NFL had always been directed by an elected president. But the position carried little power when it came to setting policy and punishing rule-breakers. NFL owners looked at baseball and its iron-fisted commissioner, Judge Kenesaw Mountain Landis (1866–1944), and decided they wanted similar leadership. Landis helped baseball rebound from the 1919 Black Sox World Series gambling scandal. His authority had organized the sport's often-bickering owners.

The NFL owners sought someone with a solid reputation and a recognizable name to do something similar. Their choice was Elmer Layden, who had been one of the famed Four Horsemen of the University of Notre Dame's Fighting Irish football team in 1924. Layden was now coaching the Fighting Irish and serving as the school's athletic director. He was just starting a new contract at the university, but the NFL brass convinced him to accept their offer to be commissioner.

Carl L. Storck had been an NFL leader since 1920 and its acting president since 1939. He wasn't thrilled about acquiring a new boss in Layden. So Storck resigned from the job.

Fantasy Football

One of the most talked-about football teams of 1941 was at Plainfield Teachers College, which piled up a number of lopsided victories behind John Chung, a sophomore halfback from China. There was just one downside to the Plainfield story: It was completely false.

The school was the creation of Morris Newburger, a Wall Street stockbroker with a little too much time on his hands. Posing as public-relations director Jerry Croyden, Newburger began calling *The New York Times* with scores and other details of Plainfield Teachers College games. (One installment explained how Chung derived strength from eating rice between quarters.) *The Times* printed the results, and other newspapers followed.

On November 13, Newburger issued a press release stating, sadly, that Chung and his teammates had flunked their midterm exams and would play no more games. Four days later, *Time* magazine revealed the hoax.

1941

One Strike Away

The 1941 World Series matchup was half-familiar to sports fans. The American League representative, Joe McCarthy's (1887–1978) New York Yankees, were making their fifth appearance in six years. But the National Leaguers, Leo Durocher's (1905–1991) Brooklyn Dodgers, hadn't been in the Series since 1920.

The subway rivals—Brooklyn is one of New York's five boroughs, as is the home borough of the Yankees, the Bronx—were evenly matched, and the first three October games were decided by one run each. The Yankees took the first game 3–2, the Dodgers claimed game two by the same score, and New York scored twice in the eighth inning against Brooklyn relief ace Hugh Casey to win the third game 2–1.

Game four, played in Ebbets Field, Brooklyn, is one that lingers in the memory of New York sports fans. Through eight innings of another tense battle, Brooklyn clung to a 4–3 lead. Casey had taken the mound again, and he promptly retired the first two Yankees (Johnny Sturm and Red Rolfe) in the ninth inning. With three balls and two strikes on New York's Tommy Henrich, the crowd stood in anticipation of a victory by the hometown Dodgers. Brooklyn catcher Mickey Owen signaled for a curveball. Of course, he wasn't sure if Casey would be throwing his sharp-breaking curve or his big looper. The pitch fooled the batter completely. Henrich, a New York outfielder, swung and missed, and umpire Larry Goetz signaled a strikeout.

Unfortunately, the pitch fooled Owen as well. The ball glanced off his mitt and shot back to the wall. If a pitch gets past the catcher on a third strike, the batter is allowed to run to first base—and that's just what Henrich did. The next man up, Joe DiMaggio, singled to left. Casey was coming undone. Before the inning was over he yielded two-run doubles to both Charlie Keller and Joe Gordon. The Yankees won 7–4 and then trampled the Dodgers 3–1 in game five to win the title.

Owen couldn't forgive himself for opening the door. "It was as good a curveball as Casey ever threw," he said. "I should have had it."

The War Comes to America

Even before the United States officially entered World War II, the conflict in Europe was taking its toll on American sports. The U.S. armed forces began drafting young men in 1940. The first regular Major League Baseball player to get the call was Hugh Mulcahy, a pitcher for the Philadelphia Phillies who had been a 20-game loser in two of his three full seasons. Mulcahy, drafted in March, missed almost five full seasons.

Many more athletes followed. In fact, by the end of 1941, 328 out of 607 major leaguers were in the military.

The involvement of athletes—and Americans from all other walks of life—spiraled upward after December 7. This was the morning Japanese planes attacked the U.S. naval base at Pearl Harbor, on the Hawaiian island of Oahu.

Because December 7 was a Sunday, several NFL games were in progress

Other Milestones of 1941

✔ The Amateur Athletic Union adopted synchronized swimming (an artistic swimming routine) as a sanctioned sport for doubles and team events. The first championship meet was held in Wilmette, Illinois, on March 1.

✔ Chicago and Green Bay tied atop the West Division and met in the first NFL divisional playoff December 14. Chicago won 33–14, then beat the New York Giants 37–9 for the league title.

NFL-champion Chicago Bears

✔ The National Collegiate Athletic Association (NCAA) basketball tournament final was broadcast nationally for the first time, by the Mutual Broadcasting Network. The University of Wisconsin defeated Washington State University, 39–34.

✔ The NFL spurned Spalding and adopted the Wilson football as its official ball. The move helped differentiate the professional game from college football.

across the country. At the Polo Grounds in New York and at Comiskey Park in Chicago, public-address announcers interrupted their patter and directed all servicemen to report to their units. At Griffith Stadium in Washington, D.C., the announcer paged high-ranking government and military officials, but he did not mention the attack.

The next day, America officially declared war against the Axis powers of Japan, Germany, and Italy.

1942

Reversal of Reversal of Fortune

The National Hockey League's Detroit Red Wings had a completely forgettable regular season, finishing fifth out of seven teams. Then the playoffs started, and they looked as if they had discovered a magic potion as they knocked off the favored Montreal Canadiens and Boston Bruins.

Detroit made it all the way to the Stanley Cup finals in April, where it ran into a Toronto Maple Leafs' team loaded with stars such as goalie Turk Broda and the great Syl Apps. No matter. The Red Wings kept rolling and went up three games to none in the seven-game series.

Playing before 13,694 crazed fans in Detroit in game four, the Maple Leafs were indeed on thin ice. The series looked to be over when the Red Wings went up 2–0 in the first period. Then Toronto regained its composure, fighting back to tie the game at 2–2 in the second period. Early in the third period, Detroit's Carl Lipscombe drilled a 35–foot slapshot that fooled Broda and put the home team up 3–2. It was Apps who bailed out the Maple Leafs this time, sneaking in front of the net

and flicking in the puck to tie it at 3–3. It was a pair of siblings who finally put Toronto on top. Don Metz passed to Nick Metz, who threaded a shot for a 4–3 lead.

The Red Wings went after Broda with a vengeance, but referee Mel Harris whistled them for four penalties in the waning minutes of the game. They couldn't make up the gap shorthanded (in hockey, when a player takes a penalty his team plays a man short). After the game ended, Detroit coach Jack Adams and his players charged Harris to argue. A brawl ensued, leading to Adams' suspension.

Heartened by the win, Toronto came back to tie the series on consecutive shutouts by Broda. The Red Wings grabbed a 1–0 lead in game seven, in front of a then-record crowd at Maple Leaf Garden. But resilient Toronto again came back, relying on two goals by Sweeney Schriner to win 3–1 and earn its first Stanley Cup in a decade. The Maple Leafs were the only NHL team of the 20th century to come back from a 3–0 deficit in the finals.

In 1945, the two teams tangled for the title again. This time, Toronto spurted to a three-game lead, only to see Detroit storm back to tie it. The Maple Leafs

Comeback Kings   *The 1942 Maple Leafs, seen here against the New York Rangers, won the Stanley Cup.*

avoided a reversal of fortune by winning another game seven.

Troubled Times

As battles raged on Midway Island in the Pacific and in North Africa, among other hot spots in World War II, the American public looked to sporting events for a sense of normalcy. But geopolitics and sports quickly started to mix.

In fact, the first day of the new year brought a shocking development. With Japanese submarines supposedly lurking in the Pacific, the U.S. government instituted an evening blackout for the West Coast. As a result, the Rose Bowl—the most prestigious college football bowl game—was moved to Durham, North Carolina. Despite its home-field advantage, on January 1, Duke University fell to Oregon State University, 20–16.

1942

Sgt. Greenberg *Detroit Tigers star Hank Greenberg was one of the first pro athletes to sign up for military service.*

Other sports were also disrupted. Neither the Indianapolis 500 auto race nor the U.S. Open golf tournament was held in 1942, nor would they be for the next three years. In the NFL, Chicago Bears owner George Halas left for the Navy on November 1, and his backup quarterback, Young Bussey, departed about the same time. Halas returned in 1945; Bussey died in action.

In Major League Baseball, stars such as the Detroit Tigers' Hank Greenberg and the Cleveland Indians' Bob Feller joined the military. (Feller's Navy enlist-ment, two days after Pearl Harbor on December 9, 1941, was broadcast live on the radio.) Some older athletes who were not eligible for the draft enlisted nonetheless, lending their names to the war effort. Charlie Gehringer, who had played 19 fine seasons with Detroit, joined the Navy at the age of 39. He ran a physical-fitness program and rose to the rank of lieutenant commander. Ted Lyons, the Chicago White Sox's top pitcher for most of his 20 seasons, enlisted in the Marines at age 42.

Play Ball!

In 1942, as Americans began to worry that the forces of fascism were overrunning the world, Major League Baseball commissioner Kenesaw Mountain Landis contacted President Franklin D. Roosevelt and offered to suspend baseball if it suited the needs of the country. Landis knew that President Woodrow Wilson had halted all "nonessential industries" near the end of World War I, cutting short the 1918 baseball season, although the World Series had gone on that year and no seasons were canceled.

Roosevelt's reply to Landis is remembered as the "Green Light Letter." It read, in part:

"I honestly feel that it would be best for the country to try to keep baseball going. There will be fewer people unemployed and everybody will work longer hours and harder than ever before. And that means that they ought to have a chance for recreation and for taking their minds off their work even more than before. . . . Here is another way of looking at it—if 300 teams use 5,000 or 6,000 players, these players are a definite recreational asset to at least 20,000,000 of their fellow citizens—and that in my judgment is thoroughly worthwhile."

Flight of the Cardinals

The St. Louis Cardinals' narrow misses were becoming all too familiar in baseball, having finished second in the National League in 1939 and 1941, and third in 1940. They seemed to take a step backward in 1942, but suddenly caught fire in mid-August and finished two games ahead of the second-place Brooklyn Dodgers (who won 102 games).

The Cardinals didn't have a lot of pop; they hit only 60 home runs as a team. But their pitching was virtually flawless, led by Mort Cooper (22–7, 10 shutouts, 1.78 ERA) and Johnny Beazley (21–6, 2.13 ERA). As a staff, St. Louis' pitchers posted a stunning ERA of 2.55. Perhaps more important, the team was managed expertly by Billy Southworth, who regularly used 13 position players and eight pitchers.

In the American League, the New York Yankees' pitching staff of Red Ruffing, Spud Chandler, Ernie Bonham, and Hank Borowy was nearly as proficient at the Cardinals'. When the two teams met in the World Series in October, most fans expected a pitching duel.

It was the veteran Ruffing who dominated game one, taking a no-hitter into the bottom of the eighth inning. He got his record seventh Series win, but the Cardinals' four runs in the bottom of the ninth inning were an omen. St. Louis took the next four games, all of them close. Outfielder Enos Slaughter scored the winning run in game two, then saved the day by throwing out a runner at third base in the ninth inning. Third baseman Whitey Kurowski's two-run homer for St. Louis struck the final blow in the ninth inning of game five. The Cardinals were World Series champions.

THE WHITE HOUSE
WASHINGTON

January 15, 1942.

My dear Judge:-

Thank you for yours of January fourteenth. As you will, of course, realize the final decision about the baseball season must rest with you and the Baseball Club owners -- so what I am going to say is solely a personal and not an official point of view.

I honestly feel that it would be best for the country to keep baseball going. There will be fewer people unemployed and everybody will work longer hours and harder than ever before.

And that means that they ought to have a chance for recreation and for taking their minds off their work even more than before.

Baseball provides a recreation which does not last over two hours or two hours and a half, and which can be got for very little cost. And, incidentally, I hope that night games can be extended because it gives an opportunity to the day shift to see a game occasionally.

As to the players themselves, I know you agree with me that individual players who are of active military or naval age should go, without question, into the services. Even if the actual quality of the teams is lowered by the greater use of older players, this will not dampen the popularity of the sport. Of course, if any individual has some particular aptitude in a trade or profession, he ought to serve the Government. That, however, is a matter which I know you can handle with complete justice.

Here is another way of looking at it -- if 300 teams use 5,000 or 6,000 players, these players are a definite recreational asset to at least 20,000,000 of their fellow citizens -- and that in my judgment is thoroughly worthwhile.

With every best wish,

Very sincerely yours,

Hon. Kenesaw M. Landis,
333 North Michigan Avenue,
Chicago,
Illinois.

Franklin D. Roosevelt

"Green Light Letter " *This letter from President Franklin Delano Roosevelt to Commissioner Landis gave Major League Baseball the "green light" to keep playing during the war years.*

Our Man in St. Louis

Watching young Stan Musial stride to the plate for another appearance at Ebbets Field, the Brooklyn Dodgers fans could only sigh, "Here comes that man again." On the road or at home in St. Louis, he became "Stan the Man," one of baseball's most beloved players.

Musial's career with the Cardinals lasted 22 seasons. Using an unconventional, corkscrewed batting stance, he was a rare combination of power and contact, a man who blasted 475 career home runs yet hit .310 or better in each of his first 16 full seasons.

Musial turned down a basketball scholarship to the University of Pittsburgh in 1938, opting to sign with the Cardinals as a left-handed pitcher. A shoulder injury ended that dream, but he got his chance as a hitter when he was called up from a minor-league team late in 1941. By 1943 he was voted Most Valuable Player of the National League.

Stan the Man retired with more than two dozen National League records. He was the first player to log 1,000 games at each of two positions—outfield and first base. He played in 24 All-Star Games (there were two per season from 1959 to 1962), and his statue now stands in front of Busch Stadium in St. Louis.

As longtime broadcaster Harry Carey said, "He was the greatest star—the character, the soul, the accessibility. Nobody combined that with as much baseball greatness as Musial."

Teddy Ballgame

He was an average fielder and not much of a runner on the base paths. But as a pure hitter, it is unlikely anyone in the last 60 years can match Ted Williams, the Boston Red Sox's "Splendid Splinter."

In 1942 Williams won the American League Triple Crown, batting .356 with 36 home runs and 137 RBI, leading the league in all three batting categories.

As a high school senior in San Diego, California, Williams stood 6-foot-3 and weighed 145 pounds. A Detroit Tigers' scout told Williams' mother that her son would probably die if he was subjected to a year in the major leagues. Fortunately for baseball fans in the 1940s and 1950s, Williams eventually gained 60 pounds and developed into a menacing presence at the plate.

His batting eye was practically perfect; it is said that his eyesight was so good he could figure out which way a pitch was spinning before he began his swing. He was a strict pull hitter (that is, as a lefthanded hitter, he hit most of his balls to right field; a righty pull hitter usually hits to left field), but would adjust his swing when absolutely necessary—such as in 1946, when he hit a ball down the third-base line and wound up with an inside-the-park home run to clinch the American League pennant. It was the only pennant the Red Sox won in his 17 full seasons with the team.

Williams' career statistics—including 521 home runs and 1,839 RBI—are doubly impressive when you consider that he lost three years fighting in World War II and most of two more as a jet fighter pilot in the Korean War. He had 145 RBI for the Red Sox at the age of 21, and he hit

.316 in 310 at-bats at the age of 42. Appropriately, he hit a home run in his final at-bat on September 28, 1960.

G.I. Joe (and Airman Ted)

The war presented an ethical dilemma for millions of Americans, including athletes. Were they needed at home, where they had families and job commitments, or should they fight for the Allies in Europe or the Pacific? Baseball's biggest stars, Joe DiMaggio and Ted Williams, both accepted deferments that kept them out of the military. The 25-year-old Williams was the sole supporter of his divorced mother, while 28-year-old DiMaggio had a wife and an infant.

But they were criticized in the newspapers and occasionally reprimanded by fans, and the pressure finally got to be too much. Soon after the end of the 1942 season, DiMaggio joined the Army as a sergeant and Williams entered Navy flight school. Each lost three prime seasons.

Williams didn't see any action in World War II, though he later flew 39 combat missions over Korea. DiMaggio's assignments primarily consisted of playing baseball for Army teams. Still, the symbolic statement carried a great impact. As New York Yankees pitcher Lefty Gomez said, "He knew he was Joe DiMaggio, and he knew what that meant to the country."

Frozen Gloves

Although athletics continued to thrive as America entered the war, the National Boxing Association con- cluded that boxing was inappropriate. So the association froze all titles on October 16 and encouraged its competitors to join the military effort, even if it was only to promote physical education, sell war bonds, or put on boxing exhibitions to lift the morale of the troops.

Joe Louis, the renowned heavyweight champion, joined the Army on January 10. While he never came close to any whizzing bullets, he proved to be a tireless and important participant. Over his four-year tour of duty, Louis traveled more than 70,000 miles and fought 96 exhibition matches. In 1944 he starred in *The Negro*

G.I. Joe *Boxer Joe Louis enlisted in the Army. He spent his service fighting not at the front, but in the ring.*

1942

Soldier, a film directed by Frank Capra that was designed to encourage African Americans to enlist in the military.

More important than the diversion he offered were the cultural changes Louis helped effect. Assigned to a base at Fort Riley, Kansas, in 1942, he met a young college football star and soldier named Jackie Robinson, who later joined Louis as one of the decade's towering sports figures. Robinson complained that he and 18 other black soldiers were being improperly denied entrance into the officer-candidate program.

Louis took up the issue with Truman Gibson, special advisor on Negro affairs to the secretary of war, and with Brigadier General Donald A. Robinson, commanding officer of the Cavalry Training Center at Fort Riley. Louis even threatened to pull out of his scheduled exhibitions, and Robinson and his comrades were admitted to officer-candidate schools within a week. All became officers.

On another occasion, a British theater denied Louis admission, explaining that the American commanding officer gave an order prohibiting his white and black soldiers from attending movies together. Louis complained, and a superior officer revoked the order. He also fired the commanding officer. "If whites and blacks were all fighting the same war," Louis asked, "why couldn't their morale be lifted at the same theater?"

Louis was honorably discharged from the Army in 1945, taking with him a Legion of Merit award for his service.

Other Milestones of 1942

✔ The NHL discontinued regular-season overtime games because of wartime blackout restrictions.

✔ Stanford University defeated Dartmouth College 53–38 to win the NCAA basketball championship in March.

✔ The Indianapolis 500 was canceled due to the war and gasoline rationing.

✔ Golfer Byron Nelson won his second Master's tournament in April, edging Ben Hogan.

✔ Swimmer Gloria Callen was the Associated Press female athlete of the year.

Frank Sinkwich

✔ Frank Sinkwich, the University of Georgia's electrifying halfback, won the Heisman Trophy, given to college football's best player. Soon after, he enlisted in the Marines.

Buckeye Fever

Boston College and Georgia Tech cruised through the 1942 season as the nation's dominant teams in college football—a sport that had not yet been undermined much by the war. Then they both got leveled. Holy Cross College surprised Boston College 55–22, and Georgia whipped intrastate rival Tech 34–0.

That opened the door for Ohio State University, which was powered by tailback Les Horvath. The Ohio State Buckeyes also lost one game in 1942, 17–7 to the University of Wisconsin. But that loss came with an asterisk. Twenty-one Ohio State players fell ill on the trip to Wisconsin. Associated Press voters took pity and made the Buckeyes number one in their final college football rankings.

Redskins' Revenge

The Chicago Bears' 73–0 romp in the 1940 NFL Championship Game propelled the team to a new level of confidence. The Bears won the title again in 1941, and looked even stronger in 1942 as they went 11–0 and outscored their opponents 376–84. The "Monsters of the Midway" seemed to be invincible in every way.

The Washington Redskins also had an impressive season in 1942, finishing 10–1. But betters made them 22-point underdogs in the 1942 Championship Game on December 13. Chicago, after all, had won 24 consecutive games, if you include postseason and preseason. Plus, nobody believed Washington could mentally recover from the historic beating it had taken two seasons earlier.

Sure enough, the Bears went up 6–0 in the second quarter, scoring when 230-pound tackle Lee Artoe picked up a fumble and ran 50 yards for a touchdown. But the Redskins stiffened. They answered the Bears with a 38-yard touchdown pass from Sammy Baugh to Wilbur Moore, then added a short plunge over the goal line by Andy Farkas in the third quarter. The underrated Washington defense didn't allow another point.

Baugh completed five of 13 passes for 66 yards, nowhere near his usual production. But the versatile star made one of the game's biggest defensive plays, intercepting a pass in the end zone.

Another Chicago drive ended on downs after officials called back a touchdown because of a penalty. "I guess this kinda makes up for that thing in 1940," Baugh said afterward.

1943

War Is Hell

🏆 By 1943, every sport in America was changed, and usually diminished, by the war. Due to the demand for rubber, for example, Major League Baseball substituted blatta, a gummy substance, for the layer of rubber that surrounds the ball's cork center. Whether because of the modified ball or because so many of the game's best hitters were in military uniform, offense sagged. In 1944, the New York Yankees' Nick Etten led the American League with a mere 22 home runs.

College football may have been hit hardest. By 1943, more than 300 colleges had abandoned the sport. Many of these were small schools with halfhearted programs. Others had proud gridiron traditions, such as the University of Alabama, Stanford University, Fordham University, and Georgetown University. Some universities fielded teams only by lifting the ban against freshman competitors.

The 1943 Army–Navy game, meanwhile, was played at the West Point (New York) Army Academy, rather than its usual big-city venue. The academy limited tickets to on-duty Army personnel and civilians living within 10 miles of the stadium. Several U.S. Congressmen protested, but under-secretary of war Robert P. Patterson remained firm, saying it was necessary "because of transportation and fuel shortages."

In the NFL, strangely familiar names began to resurface. Bronko Nagurski hadn't played in five seasons. But the Chicago Bears coaxed the legendary fullback out of retirement at the age of 34, and he helped them to their third championship in four years.

Crowned in Absentia

In 1943, no college football player could escape the shadow of "Accurate" Angelo Bertelli, dynamic quarterback of the top-ranked Fighting Irish of the University of Notre Dame. But Bertelli got his draft notice just after midseason and spent the rest of the schedule in Marine boot camp at Parris Island Marine Base in South Carolina.

Amazingly, Bertelli won the Heisman Trophy anyway. The vote wasn't even close. He was unable to attend the award ceremony on December 3, though. He was busy cleaning his rifle and doing push-ups in the dirt.

You Go, Girls *Women got their chance on the diamond during World War II with their own pro baseball league.*

Even golf, that supposed refuge of the upper class, felt the pinch. By 1943, Sam Snead, Jimmy Demaret, Lloyd Mangrum, Lawson Little, and other top golfers were in the armed forces. Mangrum, in fact, was wounded twice during the Battle of the Bulge.

Diamonds Are a Girl's Best Friend

With recognizable names disappearing from Major League Baseball rosters by the week, professional baseball was losing some of its appeal. At the same time, women's semipro and amateur softball leagues had been experiencing a decade-long boom. One estimate for 1943 placed the number of teams nationwide at 40,000. Philip K. Wrigley, owner of the Chicago Cubs, noted these two facts and started the All-American Girls Softball League, composed of the Kenosha (Wisconsin) Comets, the Racine (Wisconsin) Belles, the Rockford (Illinois) Peaches, and the South Bend (Indiana) Blue Sox.

At first, the league used a 12-inch ball and pitched it underhand. But it soon

1943

changed into true baseball, and in 1945 the league changed the word Softball in its name to Baseball. The only difference from the men's game—besides the pastel skirts—was a smaller diamond, with 72 feet between bases instead of 90. These short base paths helped Sophie Kurys steal 201 bases in 203 attempts in 1943.

This was an era when women flooded into jobs traditionally occupied by their husbands and brothers, including heavy manufacturing. Some men worried about a loss of femininity, and Wrigley insisted that his players adhere to a strictly lady-like image—as evidenced by the assertion that the AAGBL allowed "no freaks or Amazons." This theme was continued by advertising executive Arthur Meyerhoff, who purchased Wrigley's share in 1944. (Meyerhoff's Management Corporation administered the league from 1944 through 1950.)

Wrigley and Meyerhoff instructed scouts to weigh both physical appearance and ability when evaluating prospects. In spring training of 1943 and 1944, the league sent its athletes to an evening charm school conducted by Helena Rubinstein's well-known Chicago beauty salon. They were coached on subjects such as posture, fashion, applying make-up, and table manners.

A dress code distributed in 1951 read, "Masculine hair styling, shoes, coats, shirts, socks, T-shirts are barred at all times." Getting ejected from a game cost a player a $10 fine ($10 was a lot for women making $50 to $85 per week); appearing "unkempt" in public drew an even stiffer penalty. Each team had a chaperone to make sure the women did not misbehave.

"When I first started, I thought, 'Gosh, how the heck are we going to play ball in those things?'" Racine's Anna May Hutchison said of the skirts. "But once you got used to them they were just your uniform and that was it."

In general, the AAGBL was a huge hit. The league successfully expanded to small industrial centers such as Kalamazoo and Battle Creek, Michigan; Fort Wayne, Indiana; and Peoria, Illinois. (It did not fare as well in larger cities such as Chicago and Milwaukee.) Attendance grew annually until it peaked in 1948, when the 10-team league drew almost a million fans. It even spawned a rival, the National Girls Baseball League.

Popularity declined after that, however, as the novelty wore off and fans either returned to men's baseball or stayed home to watch the new medium of television. The AAGBL folded after the 1954 season. Curiously, the league that opened so many doors for female athletes was extremely slow to hire African Americans.

Sugar and the Bull

Everyone associated with boxing respected the skills of Sugar Ray Robinson, but Jake LaMotta, who spent time in reform school before entering the ring and becoming the "Bronx Bull," never feared him. The two boxers tangled six times over their careers, and each fight seemed to be bloodier and more intense than the last. "I fought Sugar so often, I almost got diabetes," LaMotta joked.

Robinson, who usually fought as a welterweight, beat LaMotta, a middleweight, in 1942. He defeated plenty of other foes, too. He was, in fact, 40–0 (with 29 knockouts) when he met LaMotta again on February 5, 1943. This time the Bronx Bull handed Robinson his first professional loss, taking a 10-round decision. Barely three weeks later, February 26, Robinson won a decision over LaMotta in another 10-rounder.

The two met twice again in 1945. And on February 14, 1951, before 15,000 fans in Chicago, welterweight champion Robinson beat middleweight champion LaMotta in a 13th-round technical knockout, claiming his second championship belt. By the end of the fight, now called the "Valentine's Day Massacre," the Bronx Bull was hardly able to raise his hands in defense.

"Jake was the toughest guy I ever fought," Robinson said. "I hit him with everything, and he'd just act like you're crazy. I never did knock him off his feet." He did, however, serve as LaMotta's best man when his rival got married late in life.

Ride 'em, Cowboys!

Basketball, especially on the high school and collegiate levels, always has been associated with the Midwest. Powerful teams had emerged on both coasts in the 1930s. But it wasn't until 1943 that the Rocky Mountain zone made its mark. The team that did it was the Cowboys of the University of Wyoming.

Unsafe at Any Weight

Long before there was a welterweight champion named Sugar Ray Leonard or a rock band called Sugar Ray, the original Sugar Ray Robinson brought life to boxing's oldest cliché of being "pound for pound" the greatest fighter ever.

He was born Walker Smith, Jr., on May 3, 1921, in the same impoverished Detroit neighborhood that produced Joe Louis. The "Ray Robinson" part came when he borrowed a friend's union card for an amateur boxing tournament. The "Sugar" came from New York City gym owner George Gainford, who tried to explain how sweet the moves of his young fighter were.

Robinson's career seemed to last forever. He fought professionally for 25 years, winning 175 fights (109 by knockout) and claiming six world championships. In 202 career fights, he failed to go the dis-

tance only once. He practically waltzed through his first 40 fights, and he won numerous contests after the age of 40.

"Robinson could deliver a knockout blow going backward," Bert Sugar wrote in *The Ring*. "His footwork was superior to any that had been seen up to that time. His speed and leverage were unmatchable."

Robinson was a flamboyant character who drove a pink Cadillac, owned a Harlem, New York, nightclub, and traveled around Europe with a large entourage that included a valet, a barber, and a mascot who was a dwarf. He made a lot of money and spent every penny of it. It is said that when the retired Robinson received a huge honorary trophy from Madison Square Garden, he didn't own a piece of furniture strong enough to support it.

The Cowboys were coached by Ev Shelton, who took over the program in 1939. Shelton won 328 games with the Cowboys, and after his death was elected to the National Basketball Hall of Fame. The 1943 squad was his crowning glory.

The team was led by Kenny Sailors, still the only player in Wyoming basketball history to earn All-America honors three times. A native of Hillsdale, Wyoming, Sailors is credited (by some, anyway) with inventing the jump shot; certainly his success helped popularize the shot (before then, players normally shot while standing on the floor). Sailors was the college basketball player of the year in 1943.

The Cowboys breezed through a 31–2 season, even though they played just nine home games. The only games they lost were to Duquesne, early in the schedule, and the Denver Legion team. They beat Regis 101–45, an unlikely score in that slow-paced era. The NCAA tournament in March proved to be a tough ride, though. Wyoming scraped by in its first two games, beating Oklahoma 53–50 and Texas 58–54. The championship game was more one-sided. The Cowboys beat Georgetown 46–34, and Sailors was named the tournament MVP.

Two days later, Wyoming faced off with St. John's University, the NIT champion, in a benefit game for the Red Cross. This one went into overtime, but Wyoming again came out on top, 52–47 in hostile Madison Square Garden in New York.

Sailors then left for two years of military service, but returned to gain further All-America recognition in 1946.

Hostilities at Home

World War II quite literally altered the landscape of Europe and East Asia, and it also brought profound changes to American society. It is estimated that 1.6 million people moved from the South to northern industrial cities, filling jobs in factories making war materials. Many of these uprooted families were African-American, and the demographic shift was not always a smooth one.

In Detroit, called the "arsenal of democracy" at the time because of its munitions plants, interracial tension heated to the boiling point. A riot erupted in June, and Briggs Stadium was right in the middle of the violence. On June 23, the Detroit Tigers and Cleveland Indians played a baseball doubleheader with 350 armed troops stationed in the stands. The next day, there were 6,617 paying customers and 2,000 troops.

The riots finally ended with 34 people dead (25 of them black, 9 white), 700 injured, and 1,200 in jail. Clearly, Nazi Germany was not the only country struggling with issues of race and identity.

The Arms Race

As the war effort began to deplete Major League Baseball rosters, the best teams were often those that could hang on to their top players. The New York Yankees lost half of their starting lineup between 1942 and 1943, but their pitching staff was largely intact. Spud Chandler mowed through American League hitters, going 20–4 with a league-best ERA of 1.64 . Starting pitchers Ernie Bonham and Hank Borowy also stayed with the Yankees.

Likewise, the St. Louis Cardinals had a fairly full complement of arms. In fact, the top three pitchers in the National

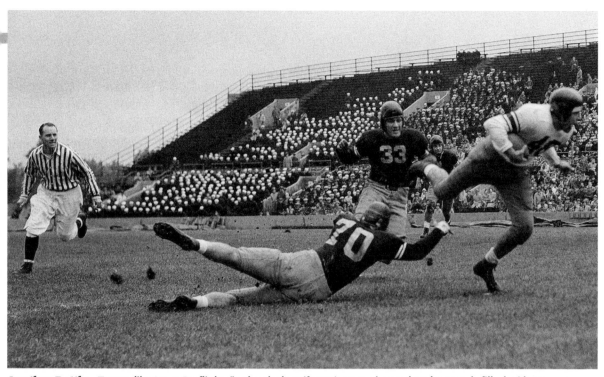

Another Battle *Teams like Iowa Preflight (in the dark uniforms) were cheered on by stands filled with Navy men.*

League in ERA were all Cardinals: Howie Pollet, Max Lanier, and Mort Cooper. Cooper went 21–8, maintaining his position as the league's most feared thrower. St. Louis also had Stan Musial, who hit .357 and racked up 220 hits.

The Yankees won the American League pennant by 13 1/2 games, the Cardinals took the National League flag by 18 games, and the two teams faced off in October in a World Series rematch.

This time, New York turned the tables. A year earlier, St. Louis committed 10 errors but still managed to win four of five games. The Cardinals made 10 errors in five games again, and this year it cost them. Compounding the defensive lapses was a lack of timely hitting; St. Louis left 37 runners on base in five games in the Fall Classic.

Chandler pitched two complete games and surrendered only one earned run. The Yankees' Marius Russo, who went 5–10 during the season, started game four, pitched a complete game, and scored the winning run when he doubled and came home on a sacrifice fly by shortstop Frankie Crosetti.

In this pitcher-dominated era, the teams combined to hit .222 in the Series.

Go Iowa Preflight!

America's coaches and military leaders were divided on the issue of college athletics. Some saw sports programs as excellent training for the rigors of war, others as an energy-wasting diversion. One supporter of college sports was Commander Tom Hamilton, head of the U.S.

1943

Navy and Marine Corps. Hamilton advocated football, in particular, as a form of combat preparation. So colleges with Naval training programs were allowed to suit up sailors in football uniforms.

What's more, many Navy and Marine bases and flight schools fielded their own teams. And they were among the best in the nation. In 1943, the Associated Press Top 20 College Football Teams included Iowa Preflight, Great Lakes Naval Station, DelMonte Preflight, March Field, and Bainbridge Navy Training School. Randolph Field tied a strong University of Texas team in the Cotton Bowl in January.

The next year, four of those teams made the Top 20 again (all but DelMonte), along with Randolph Field, Norman Preflight, El Toro Marines, Fort Pierce, St. Mary's Preflight, and Second Air Force. The 1944 bowl lineup included something called the Treasury Bowl, with Randolph Field defeating Second Air Force 13–6.

Steagles and Carpets

The NFL, like all professional sports leagues, found it increasingly difficult to build team rosters with any depth. Two teams, in particular—the Pittsburgh Steelers and their interstate rivals, the Philadelphia Eagles—were on the verge of collapse as the 1943 season approached.

So NFL owners called a special meeting and agreed to allow the two franchises to merge their talent for one season. The team was officially known as the Phil–Pitt Eagles–Steelers. Sports fans quickly dubbed them the Steagles.

Philadelphia's Earle Neale and Pittsburgh's Walt Kiesling shared the head-coaching duties. Neale directed the offense, Kiesling the defense, and they barely kept their hands off one another's throats. Neale cursed a mistake-prone Steelers' player at one practice, and Kiesling pulled all the Steelers off the field. The two coaches never became friends.

Most of the Steagles had been rejected by the armed forces for one reason or another. Running back Jack Hinkle got an early discharge because of stomach ulcers. It was a twice-broken wrist that kept Pro Bowl tackle Al Wistert out of the Army. Guard Ed Michaels was deaf in one ear. He removed his helmet in the huddle to hear the play call.

The players were required to work at least 40 hours a week in factories making armaments. They trained at the University of Pennsylvania six evenings a week. "You worked all day, and you practiced all night, and by the end of the day you were tired as hell," Hinkle said.

The Steagles were surprisingly good in 1943. Wearing the Eagles' green and white, and splitting their home games between Philadelphia's Shibe Park and Pittsburgh's Forbes Field, they went 5–4–1. Hinkle led a strong ground attack with 571 yards rushing.

The merger officially ended on the final day of the season. The Eagles flew solo in 1944 and narrowly missed the Eastern Division title with a record of 7–1–2. The Steelers, however, still needed help. This time they merged with the Chicago Cardinals, forming a conglomerate that stumbled to an 0–10 record, getting outscored 328–108 along the way. The name of this team was Card–Pitt. To fans, they would always be the Carpets.

Other Milestones of 1943

✔ Count Fleet, ridden by jockey Johnny Longden, became the sixth horse ever to win the Triple Crown, capturing the Kentucky Derby, Preakness Stakes, and Belmont Stakes—which he won by 25 lengths.

✔ Relief pitcher Ace Adams set a 20th-century record by pitching in 70 baseball games for the New York Giants. He pitched a complete game in

Johnny Longden on Count Fleet

only one of them. (The record is now held by relief pitcher Mike Marshall of the Los Angeles Dodgers, who pitched in 106 games in 1974.)

✔ In a cold, steady rain, the New York Giants and Detroit Lions battled through the NFL's last scoreless tie on November 7. Neither team's offense came inside the opponent's 15-yard line.

Triple Threat

Sammy Baugh was firmly established as the NFL's brightest star by 1943. The agile passer from Texas was, without question, the league's first great quarterback, and his Washington Redskins were title contenders every year. Yet Baugh managed to outdo himself during this season.

First he set a league record with six touchdown passes against the Brooklyn Dodgers (an NFL team from 1930 to 1944 that played under the same name as the local baseball team). Two weeks later he set another record by intercepting four passes from his safety position. Baugh wound up leading the league in passing (a completion rate of 56 percent), interceptions (11), and punting (45.9-yard average). It was a rare football Triple Crown. Longtime *Sports Illustrated* writer Peter King called it "the best season a pro football player ever had."

Baugh took Washington to the 1943 NFL Championship Game. But he got kicked in the head while making a tackle in the first half, and missed much of the game. The Chicago Bears won 41–21 on December 26.

1944

Beating the Bushes

As World War II reached its dramatic height with the bombing of Tokyo in April and Allied forces' landing on the French beach of Normandy on June 6, the sports scene at home was increasingly grim. Major League Baseball, in particular, suffered from a noticeable lack of top talent.

Only 40 percent of the players who had started on Opening Day of 1941 were around to do the same in 1944. All nine of the New York Yankees' 1941 starters had gone to war. The search for new talent was epitomized by the St. Louis Browns' signing of catcher Frank Mancuso, who had already been discharged from the Army because of a back injury (suffered while learning to do parachute jumps). Mancuso was unable to look straight into the sky for a pop-up fly ball.

Many teams welcomed back aging stars. Once-speedy outfielder Johnny Martin returned to the St. Louis Cardinals for 40 games at the age of 40. He hit .279 after a three-year absence. Jimmie Foxx (1907–1967), one of the all-time great hitters, rejoined the Chicago Cubs after a one-year layoff. The next year he even pitched for the Philadelphia Phillies. One measure of the talent drain during the war: Foxx posted a very low ERA of 1.59 in 22 2/3 innings.

Going to the other end of the age spectrum, the Cincinnati Reds put a 15-year-old pitcher on the mound. Joe Nuxhall's first appearance was about what you would expect from a kid too young to drive—five runs and five walks surrendered in two-thirds of an inning. Nuxhall didn't appear in another major league game for eight years, but then fashioned a solid pro career, mostly with the Reds.

Melancholy about the sad state of baseball, J.G. Taylor Spink of *The Sporting News* wrote to President Franklin Delano Roosevelt and suggested special considerations for baseball players. But Kenesaw Mountain Landis, the baseball commissioner, quickly informed General Lewis B. Hershey, director of the selective service, that the league sought no preferential treatment. He felt any favors would cause "bitter public resentment" and damage the reputation of baseball.

Alva Bradley, owner of the Cleveland Indians, agreed with Spink. He urged his fellow team owners to suspend operations in 1944, and for the remainder of the

A Separate Game *Forced into internment camps, Japanese Americans still played baseball (page 44).*

war, describing the baseball of the era as "a low form of comedy." The other owners sternly shot down the idea.

Oiling the Fighting Machine

Sporting events and athletes became more than diversions as the war progressed. Baseball players started visiting factories to fire up the workers and promote the sale of war bonds. Major and minor league teams welcomed sol-diers to games free of charge; by 1945, some 4.5 million soldiers had attended. Some teams sponsored "salvage days," admitting fans for free if they brought scrap metal, kitchen fat, or scrap paper.

At the same time, the country's best athletic equipment was being "drafted." In January of 1943, *The New York Times* reported that 75 percent of all new sports equipment was going to military personnel. By August of 1944, the figure rose to 90 percent, representing $20 million worth of sports supplies.

1944

At Major League Baseball stadiums, foul balls were often retrieved and sent to military bases to be used by soldiers. Commissioner Landis got an equipment fund going with a $25,000 collection, and the proceeds from the 1942 All-Star Game boosted the fund. It helped provide bats, balls, and other equipment for our fighting men and women.

Beware the Blitz

The University of Utah basketball team had no shortage of hurdles to overcome during the 1943–44 season. The players were young (most of them under 19 years old) and not particularly tall (averaging six feet). They also had no conference (it had dissolved during the war) and no gymnasium (the Army took it over), which forced the Utes to practice in local church gyms.

They overcame all of it with flair, and pretty soon people were calling them the Blitz Kids. After charging through a regular-season schedule that included many armed-forces teams, Utah declined an NCAA tournament bid and joined a strong field in the National Invitation Tournament (NIT). There they fell to University of Kentucky, 46–38 on March 26.

The Utes weren't finished in 1944, though. When the University of Arkansas bowed out of the NCAA tournament in March, organizers again invited Utah. This time the school accepted, and it rolled to the title game, where it outlasted Dartmouth College 42–40.

But even that was not the end of the season. A Red Cross benefit game in April paired the champions of each tourna-

ment. So Utah got a shot at St. John's University, which had won the NIT. The Utes won 43–36, led by freshman All-American Arnie Ferrin's 17 points.

It was a strange path to the top of the college basketball world, but Utah was happy to be there.

Baseball in the Camps

In 1944, baseball was the game that best defined and united Americans. It was an ironic and poignant twist, then, that baseball flourished in a most unlikely place—the internment camps built for Japanese Americans.

Fueled by shrill newspaper commentaries, racism, and a general feeling of paranoia, President Roosevelt signed Executive Order 9066 in February 1942, which mandated the mass eviction and incarceration of all people of Japanese descent living on the West Coast. By October of that year, most of these American citizens had been assigned to 10 internment camps—infamous and desolate places such as Manzanar and Tule Lake in California, and Gila River in Arizona.

Baseball was extremely popular in Japan, and had long been important in the Japanese-American community, so the detainees immediately set about constructing fields and ordering equipment from mail-order catalogs.

"Right near our block was an open space, so we started digging out the sagebrush from the desert floor," recalled Howard Zenimura, whose father, Kenichi, designed the baseball diamond at Gila River. "Pretty soon people came by to ask us what we were doing. We told them we

vere building a ballpark, and then everybody was out there with their shovels
learing that space."

Most of the diamonds were actually
built outside the barbed wire of the camps.
With hundreds of miles of desert in every
direction, it did not seem to matter.) Some
camp teams were allowed to travel for
exhibition games, while others welcomed
teams from outside the camps. The games
were highlights of an otherwise dreary
existence.

There were 32 teams, split among
three divisions, at Gila River alone. The
Tule Lake Baseball Convention, which
began May 2, 1944, attracted more than
,000 fans.

Of course, devotion to baseball was
not the only example of Japanese-Amer-
can loyalty. The 100th Infantry Battal-
on, made up of second-generation Nisei
from Hawaii, was among the most deco-
ated U.S. Army units of its size.

Meet Me in St. Louis

If the wartime manpower shortage
lowered the level of Major League
baseball play, at least it leveled the play-
ng field. And that was good news for the
St. Louis Browns, the American League's
most downtrodden team.

Entering the 1944 season, the Browns
had enjoyed exactly one winning year in
their last 14. During the 1930s they had
lost 90 or more games in eight of 10 years.
In 1944 the St. Louis players averaged
nearly 32 years of age. The Browns had no
stars. Yet by season's end they had edged
the Detroit Tigers by a game and won the
A.L. pennant.

With the Cardinals claiming their
third straight National League pennant,
the World Series became an all-St. Louis
affair. Opposing managers Billy Southworth (Cardinals) and Luke Sewell
(Browns), because of the wartime housing
shortage, actually shared an apartment. All
six games were played in October at
Sportsman's Park.

The Browns played tough and took a
lead of two games to one. After that, Harry
"The Cat" Breechen and the splendid Mort
Cooper pitched complete games for the
Cardinals to win games four and five, and
reliever Ted Wilks retired the last 11
Browns in the sixth game. Where the Cardinals' defense had abandoned them
against the Yankees in 1942 and 1943,
this time they made only one error, while
it was the American Leaguers who committed 10.

The Browns returned to their losing
ways by 1946, and remained in or near the
basement until moving to Baltimore and
becoming the Orioles in 1954.

Kids Behaving Badly

College basketball was steadily gaining popularity in the mid-1940s. But
the game was rocked on October 2 when
Forrest C. "Phog" Allen (1885–1974) of the
University of Kansas, one of the nation's
most respected coaches, charged that organized gamblers were inducing college
basketball players to throw games (that is,
to lose intentionally) or shave points (win,
but score fewer points—often a benefit to
gamblers). Allen warned of "a scandal
that will stink to high heaven." But college
presidents took no action.

1944

The Kansas coach was right. In January 1945, five Brooklyn College players admitted to accepting bribes. In time, four other New York-area colleges were hit by similar accusations. And it wasn't just a Big Apple problem. Bradley University (in Peoria, Illinois) and University of Toledo (in Ohio) eventually got sucked into the scandal, followed by the mighty University of Kentucky in 1951.

By the time the sport was cleaned up, eight colleges and about 40 players were implicated.

Invincible Army

While most colleges struggled mightily to assemble teams out of 4-Fs (people rejected from the military because of physical problems) and teenagers, the U.S. Military Academy (Army) had a distinct advantage. If an active serviceman had previous college playing experience, the academy could offer him three more years of athletic eligibility and keep him out of the draft until graduation. In exchange, the athletes were required to cram their four-year officers training into three years. Few could resist the deal.

These uneven standards gave Army a powerful team in an era of shaky squads and the result was fearsome to behold.

The Black Knights of Army, coached by Colonel Earl "Red" Blaik (1897–1989) simply crushed the opposition in 1944. They trounced Villanova University 83–0, chewed up Coast Guard 76–0, and mashed University of Pittsburgh 62–7. The University of Notre Dame was the defending national champion, a team that hadn't lost to Army since 1931, but the Black Knights beat the Fighting Irish 59–0 (Notre Dame's worst loss ever).

The Black Knights' biggest test came against archrival Navy, which entered the game ranked second after Army. More than 66,000 fans filled Baltimore's Municipal Stadium for the December 2 game, raising millions of dollars for war bonds. The game was close until the fourth quarter, when fullback Felix "Doc" Blanchard (b.1924) powered one touchdown drive and halfback Glenn Davis (b.1924) capped another with a 50-yard sprint. Army prevailed 23–7.

Army was so loaded with talent in 1944 that Blanchard and Davis—known as "Mr. Inside and Mr. Outside"—were not in the regular starting lineup. As freshmen they left that honor to the upperclassmen. Still, they got enough carries to rush for 1,002 yards between them, and Davis set an NCAA record with 20 touchdowns in a single season.

Two-Armed Tigers

Like Randy Johnson and Curt Schilling of baseball's Arizona Diamondbacks in recent seasons, The Detroit Tigers' Paul "Dizzy" Trout and Hal Newhouser were an unstoppable one-two pitching combination in 1944. Newhouser had a 29–9 record with an ERA of 2.22. Trout's numbers were 27–14 and 2.12. Together they combined for a staggering 664 innings and 58 complete games.

Alas, no other Tigers' pitcher even had a winning record in 1944, and the team finished one game out of first place.

Other Milestones of 1944

✔ The NCAA/AAU (Amateur Athletic Union) Joint Basketball Rules Committee outlawed goaltending—interfering with a shot after the ball has begun the downward part of its arc toward the basket—unless the shot is clearly short of the basket.

✔ Robert Hamilton, a relative unknown, beat golf legend Byron Nelson by a shot in the PGA Championship tournament in August.

Curly Lambeau

✔ On June 10, a rare triple tie ended a horse race at the Aqueduct race track in Long Island, New York. Bossuet, Brownie, and Wait a Bit crossed the finish line simultaneously in the Carter Handicap.

✔ The NFL legalized coaching from the bench. Before the change, coaches (such as Curly Lambeau of Green Bay, pictured at left) could not yell instructions to their players on the field.

Curtis Swims to the Top

It was the nuns of Ursuline Convent School in Santa Rosa, California, who taught Ann Curtis how to swim. Curtis was born in 1926, and by the age of 11 she won a freestyle race for girls under 16 organized by the Amateur Athletic Union (AAU).

Her mother held her out of major adult competition until 1943. That year, when Curtis joined the Crystal Plunge Club of San Francisco coached by the famed Charlie Sava, her career took off.

In 1944 she won the AAU national outdoor swimming championships in the 100 meters, the 400 meters, the 800 meters, and the one mile. Indoors she claimed the 220-yard and 440-yard races.

Curtis was a national sensation at the age of 18, and the AAU acknowledged it by awarding her the 1944 Sullivan Award (named for James E. Sullivan, who founded the AAU in 1888) for outstanding athletic performance and sportsmanship. She was the first female athlete to win the award since its inception in 1930, and she'd be the only one to claim the honor until diver Patricia McCormick in 1956. She also was named female athlete of the year by Associated Press in 1944.

The only thing that took away from Curtis' amazing year was the cancellation of the 1944 Summer Olympics in London. She would have been a huge favorite to win several gold medals.

Curtis would get her chance in London in 1948. She made the most of it, swimming to a gold medal in the 400-meter freestyle and a silver in the 100 meters, not to mention a gold in the 4x100 freestyle relay.

Curtis' 31 national championships stood as a record for women until Tracy Caulkins broke it in 1981.

1945

War and Peace

By 1945, the tide of World War II had turned in favor of the Allied forces. But the fighting remained heavy early in the year, and the toll back home was as severe as ever.

Major League Baseball was dealt a historic blow when the 1945 All-Star Game was canceled at the government's request. Home-grown talent was thinner than ever, with 509 of 565 active players serving in the military. The Washington Senators started three Cuban players regularly, and also had an Italian and a Venezuelan player. All of the Senators' five starting pitchers were knuckleballers—a pitch that requires less physical strength.

Meanwhile, the Brooklyn Dodgers signed Floyd "Babe" Herman, a one-time star who hadn't played in eight seasons (he was now 42). Hod Lisenbee pitched in 31 games for the Cincinnati Reds in 1945, at the age of 46. He hadn't taken the mound since 1936.

The Detroit Tigers were jokingly called the Nine Old Men. They averaged nearly 35 years in age, which didn't prevent them from beating the Chicago Cubs in October in a rather sloppily played World Series.

But none of the stories epitomized the lean mid-40s better than that of Pete Gray. The outfielder appeared in 77 games for the St. Louis Browns, hitting .218 and striking out only 11 times in 234 at-bats. Not bad for a man with one arm.

Playing Over There

For nearly four years, America's fighting forces obtained hope and relief from the stress of battle through spectator sports. As the war wound down, some of those soldiers got their own opportunities to play ball.

Soon after the liberation of Rome on June 4, 1944, for example, officials organized a Spaghetti Bowl football game. Less than three weeks after Japan signed articles of surrender aboard the *USS Missouri* on September 2, officially ending World War II, *The New York Times* announced that the winner of the Mediterranean Theater baseball championship would meet the winner of the European Theater in a best-of-five series. And in October the 508th Parachute Regiment met a U.S. Air Force team in a football game

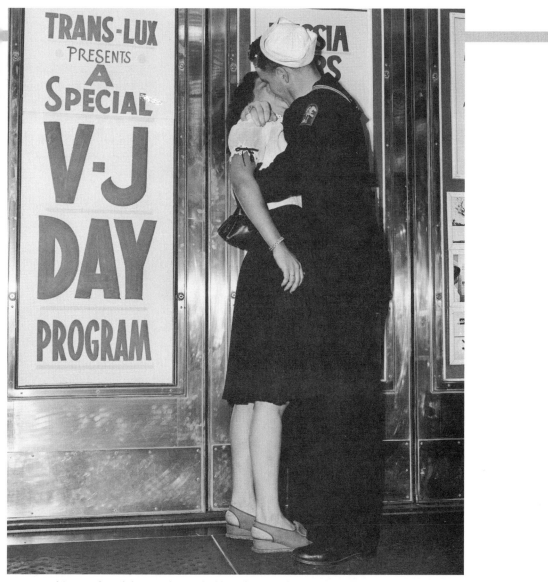

Peace *This couple celebrates the end of hostilities in the East: Victory in Japan (V-J) Day.*

held in Frankfurt on the Main, Germany. Some 20,000 soldiers were on hand to watch the action.

Many American soldiers remained in Europe even after the war was over, leading to further sporting events in 1946. The Spaghetti Bowl returned, this time in Florence, where it attracted 25,000 specta-tors. There was also a GI World Series for the championship of occupied Germany, with the 60th Infantry Regiment of the 9th Division winning four of six games against the 508th Parachute Regiment. Righthander Carl Scheib won two games in the GI World Series, then went on to win 45 games with the Philadelphia Athletics.

1945

The ultimate expression of sports-as-triumph came in 1945, though. That was when soldiers etched a baseball diamond into the field of Nuremberg Stadium, where huge Nazi rallies had so recently honored Adolph Hitler.

Bob the Big Boy

In an era when many basketball centers stood 6-foot-5 or 6-foot-6, 7-footer Bob Kurland was a giant among men. The NCAA had outlawed his goaltending defense in 1944 (see page 47), but Kurland was smooth enough to adjust.

In 1945, Oklahoma A&M coach Hank Iba (1904–1993) assembled enough talent around his big man to make a serious NCAA tournament run. (Iba coached at the school, later known as Oklahoma State University, for 35 years.) The A&M Aggies beat the University of Utah, the defending champion, in the first round, and eventually knocked off New York University 49–45 in March. Kurland was named most valuable player of the tournament. More important to the future of the sports highlight reel, he threw down the first authenticated slam dunk. He called it his "duffer shot."

After that came a Red Cross benefit game, pitting Oklahoma A&M against the NIT champion, De Paul University. This was the game fans had hoped for all year, because it matched Kurland against another agile center, George Mikan (b.1924). More than 18,000 people filed into Madison Square Garden in New York in April to witness the "Battle of the Goons." But Mikan fouled out after only 14 minutes, dousing the spectacle. Kurland scored a very mortal 14 points, and the Aggies won 52–44.

Oklahoma A&M was even better the following year, when five war veterans came home to join the five returning starters. Kurland led the team in scoring, had 72 points in three tournament games, and sparked a 43–40 victory over University of North Carolina in the NCAA final in March. The Aggies were the first college basketball team ever to win consecutive NCAA championships.

He Shoots . . . He Scores! *Maurice Richard (shown here scoring several years later) rewrote the hockey record books with his amazing goal-a-game pace in the 1944–45 season.*

One a Game

Maurice Richard's blazing goal scoring for the Montreal Canadiens in the 1944 NHL postseason (see page 42) had made him a folk hero in Quebec. All

The Mahatma

Like many maverick thinkers, Branch Rickey was a bundle of contradictions, giving equal weight to moral conduct and his desire to earn a dollar. Raised in a strict Methodist home in Ohio, he promised his father he'd never visit a ballpark on Sunday. He kept his promise, too, although he later invented the Sunday doubleheader.

That wasn't Rickey's only innovation. As the general manager of the St. Louis Cardinals, he sculpted baseball's intricate farm system, where developing players could hone their skills before joining a major-league team. He also dreamed up batting cages, sliding pits, and Ladies' Day. And after purchasing the Brooklyn Dodgers, he set about plotting the demise of the color barrier that had kept African Americans out of Major League Baseball for nearly half a century.

Never without a cigar or a witty rejoinder, the man called "the Mahatma" left a vast imprint on the game. "I really believe that in breaking down the color barrier in baseball, our 'national game,' he did more for the Negroes than any white man since Abraham Lincoln," Jackie Robinson wrote.

over the province, kids now wore his number-9 jersey and greased their hair so they would look just like the Rocket.

In 1945, Richard stretched his remarkable performance over an entire regular season. He exhausted defenders and skillfully handled the passes of his Canadiens teammates Toe Blake and Elmer Lach, lighting up scoreboards from Chicago to Boston. Richard scored his record-breaking 44th goal in his 40th game of the season.

Going into the last game of the season, he had 49 goals. The March 18 contest was broadcast by radio across Canada and followed by dispatch among Canadian soldiers abroad. Richard scored one goal against the Boston Bruins and finished with 50 goals in 50 games—something no man had done since the modern NHL was established in 1926.

It would, in fact, be the only one-goal-a-game pace over an NHL season until Wayne Gretzky (b.1961) repeated the feat in the 1981–82 season.

The New York Sports Exchange

With the national pastime so significantly affected by the war, owning a Major League Baseball team was suddenly a dubious business proposition. In New York, center of the baseball universe, two of the city's three teams traded hands in 1945. (The Giants were the exception.)

On January 26, Edward G. Barrow and the heirs of Jacob Ruppert sold the Yankees to a syndicate headed by Lawrence MacPhail (1890–1975) that included Daniel Topping and Del Webb. The price was estimated at a whopping $2.8 million. On August 10, another group of investors bought the Dodgers, with Branch Rickey (1881–1965), Walter O'Malley (1903–1979), and John L. Smith getting the controlling interest. Rickey eventually made make history as the club president, and the O'Malleys retained ownership for decades.

Saved from the Sand *Golfer Byron Nelson blasts out of a sand trap at the Riviera Country Club during the 1945 Los Angeles Open, one of an amazing 19 tournaments he won in his record-setting year.*

Full Nelson

Many of the nation's best golfers wound up fighting in World War II. Byron Nelson (b.1912) was not one of them. He was a hemophiliac, prone to excessive bleeding, and so was considered unfit for duty.

With the field diminished during the late stages of the conflict overseas, Nelson dominated the fairways as few golfers have. In 1944 he won seven tournaments, claimed more prize money than any other golfer, and averaged a crisp 69.67 strokes in 85 rounds of tournament play.

As great as that was, Nelson managed to get even better in 1945. The Texan won 19 of 31 tournaments, including 11 straight. His average for 120 tournament rounds was 68.33 strokes. He shot a blistering 62 in Seattle, Washington, tying an 18-hole tournament record, and broke the 72-hole mark with a 259.

Aging with Grace

Babe Didrikson had long ago captivated sports fans with her performance at the 1932 Olympics in Los Angeles, where she won gold medals in the javelin and 80-meter hurdles, and a silver in the high jump. She also played basketball and softball during various stages of her career.

As she got older, Didrikson increasingly turned her attention to golf. Not surprisingly, she soon established herself as the best female golfer in the world. In 1945 she began a string of dominant play that would bring her three consecutive Associated Press Woman Athlete of the Year awards.

She also hinted that she might play golf in the all-male U.S. Open. Reporters gobbled it up, and men were so spooked that the U.S. Golf Association quickly assembled a meeting and explicitly barred women from the event. Officials then changed the name of the tournament to the U.S. Men's Open. Didrikson later told friends she was only joking.

Inside, Outside, Winning Side

Anyone expecting the Army football team to fall back to earth was sorely disappointed. If anything, the Black Knights got better. Six of their opponents wound up in the final Associated Press Top 20, but the Knights treated them with no respect. The 1945 ledger included scores such as 61–0 over eighth-ranked University Pennsylvania, 54–0 over 19th-ranked Wake Forest University, and 48–0 over ninth-ranked University of Notre Dame. Over the course of two seasons, Army outscored its foes 916–81.

In 1945, halfback Glenn Davis and fullback Doc Blanchard fully took control of the backfield. Blanchard (the 205-pound "Mr. Inside," see page 45) had played for the University of North Carolina (UNC) freshman squad in 1942. He tried to get into UNC's Navy V-12 program, but bad eyesight (a mud pie nailed him in the eye as a child) and a weight problem made him ineligible. The Army drafted him in 1943 and accepted him at West Point a year later. Blanchard ran for 718 yards, scored 19 touchdowns, leveled defenders with his crushing blocks, and won the Heisman Trophy in 1945. He also became the first football player to capture the Sullivan Award.

"Have just seen Superman in the flesh," one Notre Dame coach cabled back to South Bend, Indiana, after watching Army thrash Notre Dame in 1944. "He wears number 35 and goes by the name of Blanchard."

Davis ("Mr. Outside") was an all-around athlete from Southern California who was recruited by several Major League Baseball teams. He went to West Point as a freshman in 1943, after the academy promised to also take his twin brother. Davis was then expelled for academic problems, but was readmitted after completing a special four-month math class. His blazing speed helped him rack

A Woman for All Seasons

Someone once asked Mildred "Babe" Didrikson (1915–1956) if there was anything she didn't play. "Yeah," she answered, "dolls."

It sometimes seemed that Didrikson could pick up any piece of sporting equipment and master it in a day. She was a champion runner, jumper, javelin thrower, and golfer in various stages of her career, always staying a step ahead of the pack.

At a time when "lady athletes" were expected to be sweet-natured, courteous, perhaps a little flirtatious, Didrikson was a true competitor. She flaunted and celebrated her athletic prowess and made little attempt to look pretty. And she took a beating for it, from a disapproving press that repeatedly questioned her lack of femininity.

In a supposedly supportive story about the athlete after her marriage to wrestler George Zaharias in 1935, Life magazine described a younger Didrikson as a girl whose "lips were too thin and her Adam's apple too big," and someone who "hated girls and only lived to beat them."

Didrikson didn't seem to care much. In fact, she loved the spotlight. A golfer who won 10 major tournaments, she was instrumental in founding the Ladies Professional Golf Association (LPGA) in 1949. The next year, the Associated Press voted her the Female American Athlete of the Half-Century. (Jim Thorpe was her male counterpart.) Didrikson contracted cancer and died in 1956, at the age of 45.

1945

up 944 rushing yards and 18 touchdowns in 1945, although he would have to wait for 1946 to earn his Heisman.

Army was involved in one close contest in 1945. Giving in to popular demand, Coach Red Blaik let his A and B squads go at one another for 30 minutes of inspired competition at a practice in November. They scored three touchdowns each, but Blaik cut short the exhibition when All-America tackle DeWitt "Tex" Coulter tackled Davis at the sideline and drove him into a tackling dummy.

The Patient Putter

Chick Evans was one of America's first great golfers. He won the Chicago Amateur tournament in 1907, at the age of 17, repeated the feat the next year, and

Happy Hour

Until the mid-1940s, Kenesaw Mountain Landis was the only commissioner baseball ever knew, holding the office for 24 years (from 1920 to 1944). He was a towering figure who steered the Major Leagues through everything from the Black Sox betting scandal to World War II player shortages.

When Landis died on November 25, 1944, it left the sport with a sizable power vacuum. The man the team owners selected to fill the hole was 46-year-old A.B. "Happy" Chandler (1898–1991), the former Kentucky governor and U.S. Senator. But the team owners felt he favored the players too much, and he was ousted after his seven-year term in 1951. Still, that was enough time for Chandler to oversee the revolution of African Americans playing in Major League Baseball.

won it again in 1911. In 1916 Evans became the first man to win the U.S. Open and U.S. Amateur in the same years. By 1945 he was a respected old-timer—and, in his mind, still a worthy competitor.

Evans shocked the gallery by returning to the Chicago Amateur, site of his breakthrough, and winning the tournament in 1944. Now, at the age of 55, he made it back-to-back victories.

But the great golfer would ultimately be best known for establishing the Evans Caddie Scholarships, financing the education of thousands of caddies (the people who carry a tournament player's golf clubs).

Doink!

An hour before the first postwar NFL Championship Game, played December 16 game at Cleveland Municipal Stadium, the thermometer read three degrees below zero. By kickoff, that had climbed to a relatively balmy six degrees. Hoping to keep the field thawed, groundskeepers had scattered 9,000 bales of hay on the turf, creating four feet of insulation. They swept the hay to the sidelines just before pregame warm-ups. A few minutes into the game, however, the field was frozen solid.

The game pitted the hometown Rams against the Washington Redskins. "It was like trying to play on a paved surface," Washington quarterback Sammy Baugh said. "Like we were out in the street."

Baugh had bruised his ribs two weeks earlier. Now he and his counterpart, rookie quarterback Bob Waterfield (who was married to movie star Jane Russell), tried

Other Milestones of 1945

✔ The Hockey Hall of Fame opened in Toronto, Ontario. Howie Morenz (right) was one of nine players elected as the Hall's first class of inductees.

✔ The NFL's Chicago Cardinals beat the Chicago Bears 16–7 on October 14, ending their record 29-game losing streak. The Cardinals then promptly lost their last six games of the season.

Howie Morenz

✔ University of Michigan football coach Herbert "Fritz" Crisler introduced the platoon system, sending out different squads to play offense and defense against Army.

✔ The Rockford Peaches won the championship of the All-American Girls Baseball League, which had switched from softball this season.

to deal with a vicious wind that blew off Lake Erie and prevented everyone from getting a solid grip on the ball. Players on the benches draped blankets over their legs to stave off numbness.

The game's pivotal play came early. The Redskins had just stopped Cleveland at the five-yard line when Baugh dropped back into his own end zone and fired a pass. Instead of arcing downfield, however, it clanged into one of the goal posts—which were set on the goal lines in those days. The officials ruled it a safety (when an offensive player is downed in his own end zone). Baugh and Washington head coach Dudley DeGroot argued their case, but it was the correct call according to the NFL rulebook of the day. The Rams went up 2–0.

Early in the second quarter, DeGroot took Baugh out of the game. The great

passer's injuries had only gotten worse, and he had completed just one of six passes.

Baugh's replacement, Frankie Filchock, was no slouch. He led the NFL in completions (84) and touchdown passes (13) in 1944, and he quickly connected with Steve Bagarus for a touchdown. Waterfield responded with a 37-yard touchdown pass to end Jim Benton. The teams swapped scoring passes in the third quarter. Waterfield missed an extra point, but his team maintained a tight 15–14 lead.

And that's how it ended. The Redskins twice got close enough for Joe "Hot Toe" Aguirre to attempt fourth-quarter field goals, but even his toes had gone cold. Cleveland won its first championship. A month later, the NFL rule book was revised. In the future, any pass that hit the goal post would be ruled incomplete.

1946

Calverley to the Rescue

University of Rhode Island guard Ernie Calverley weighed only 145 pounds, but he became larger than life in the 1946 NIT basketball tournament in March. In the first round, the Rhode Island Rams trailed Bowling Green State University with only a few seconds left when Calverley launched a desperation shot from 55 feet away. Bull's eye! The incredible shot tied the score, and Rhode Island went on to win 82–79 in overtime.

The unheralded Rams then knocked off Muhlenberg College to reach the tournament final against the University of Kentucky. Again Rhode Island played above its head, and in the waning moments the game was tied 45–45. This time, however, Kentucky's Ralph Beard—one of the finest players of his era—drew a foul with seconds to go, hit one free throw, and gave the Wildcats the championship.

A Black-and-White Plan

When Branch Rickey bought into the Brooklyn Dodgers in 1945 (see page 51), his main goals were to field a competitive team and to make some money. But he also had a private agenda. He wanted to break the silent but powerful color barrier that had kept African Americans out of Major League Baseball since the turn of the century.

Rickey wasn't the only man with such aspirations. Bill Veeck, Jr., a maverick owner from the start, had planned to buy the Philadelphia Phillies and fill the roster with black players in 1943, but had been blocked by Kenesaw Mountain Landis, Major League Baseball's segregationist commissioner.

In 1945, *People's Voice* sportswriter Joe Bostic ambushed Rickey, demanding a tryout for two black players he had escorted to the Dodgers' training camp. A week after that, the Boston Red Sox—pressured by a city councilman and another writer—gave auditions to three Negro League players. None of the athletes ever heard from the teams.

But Rickey, respected throughout the major leagues, was in a unique position to see it through, and he had tacit support from Happy Chandler, the new baseball commissioner (see page 54). All Rickey needed was the perfect player.

The Dodgers' boss knew that whomever he selected would be subjected to

Almost Unstoppable   *Running back Marion Motley (page 63) was among the first African Americans in the NFL, as well as one of the greatest players of all time.*

blinding public scrutiny and abuse on and off the field. Many players and countless fans would be rooting for him to fail. Rickey needed someone above reproach. He chose Jackie Robinson (1919–1972), shortstop for the Kansas City Monarchs of the Negro American League.

The grandson of a slave, raised by a single mother in Pasadena, California, Robinson had been one of the nation's top collegiate athletes, becoming UCLA's first four-letter man and excelling at baseball, football, basketball, and track. (He also found time to win the Pacific Coast

1946

Man with a Plan *Branch Rickey changed the face of baseball—and America—by signing Jackie Robinson.*

exploded. 'Robinson,' he said, 'I am looking for a ball player with guts enough not to fight back.'"

Robinson swore he could handle the job, and he was soon playing for the Dodgers' AAA team in Montreal. He led the International League with a .349 batting average and took the Royals to the 1946 minor league title, scoring the deciding run in the final game against Louisville of the American Association. Robinson had started down the road, but no one was sure where it would lead.

They Got a Football

Pro football once seemed seedy and decidedly less appealing than the college game. Lately, though, it was attracting attention—and paying customers—and some wanted to get into the fraternity. Among them were actor Don Ameche, oilman James Brueil, and lumber baron Anthony Morabito.

When the NFL shut the door on them, these three men met with other financial bigwigs at a meeting organized by Arch Ward (1896–1955), sports editor of the *Chicago Tribune*, on June 4, 1944. They came away with plans for a rival league, the All-America Football Conference.

In addition to the teams controlled by Ameche in Los Angeles (the ownership group included movie mogul Louis B. Mayer), Brueil in Buffalo, New York, and Morabito in San Francisco, the original AAFC included teams in Cleveland, New York City, Chicago, Brooklyn, and Miami.

Desperate for publicity, the new league named Jim Crowley—like NFL boss Elmer Layden, one of the legendary

intercollegiate golf championship). He also had served in the Army, where he was court-martialed, then acquitted, for challenging the segregation of an Army bus at Fort Hood, Texas. Most agreed that Robinson was not the best player in the Negro Leagues. But he was very good, he didn't smoke or drink, and he was a true soldier in the war against the segregation laws that kept the United States divided by race.

As the story goes, Rickey interviewed Robinson, informed him of the plan, then proceeded to launch an increasingly vile series of racial taunts, testing the ballplayer's resolve. As Robinson wrote in his autobiography, "'Mr. Rickey,' I asked, 'are you looking for a Negro who is afraid to fight back?' I never will forget the way he our Horsemen of Notre Dame (a group of four players given that famous nickname as collegians)—as its commissioner and baseball legend Lou Gehrig's widow, Eleanor, as the league's secretary and treasurer.

The AAFC received some bulletin-board material (that is, quotes in the newspaper that would serve to enrage or inspire an opponent) in August 1945, when Layden suggested the AAFC "first get a ball, then make a schedule, and then play a game." Miffed AAFC officials shortened the phrase to "tell them to get a ball first," and repeated it often.

By 1946, the new league had plenty of on-field talent, including more than 100 players with NFL experience, and 40 of the 66 College All-Stars of 1945 (this was a postseason team named by the Associated Press until 1976).

The AAFC's inaugural game was on September 6. More than 60,000 fans came to Cleveland Municipal Stadium to see the Browns host the ill-fated Miami Seahawks. The final score—a 44–0 whipping by the Browns—was a sign of events to come. Harvey Hester's Seahawks, stocked exclusively with Southern boys, went 3–11, wound up $80,000 in debt, and were booted from the league.

The Browns, on the other hand, were a raging success on and off the field. Coached by the brilliant Paul Brown (1908–1991), and loaded with stars such as future Hall of Fame quarterback Otto Graham (b.1921) and ends Dante Lavelli and Mac Speedie, they went 12–2 and beat the New York Yankees (named for the baseball team) in the first AAFC Championship Game.

A Moment's Hesitation

For baseball fans, the 1946 season must have seemed like waking from a bad dream. The familiar players who had steadily been drafted away from the game were back, most of them taking their old spots in the lineup. The Boston Red Sox were thrilled to get reacquainted with Ted Williams, slick-fielding second baseman Bobby Doerr, shortstop Johnny Pesky (born John Paveskovich, he had once shined Doerr's shoes as a clubhouse boy in Portland, Oregon), and center-fielder Dom DiMaggio (Joe's younger brother).

Williams pounded American League pitching for a .342 batting average and 38 home runs. Apparently he was unaffected by the rise of the "Boudreau Shift." Conceived by Cleveland Indians manager Lou Boudreau during a doubleheader in which Williams drove in 11 runs, it

Star of Stars

Despite his many honors, Ted Williams was always driven to prove himself. Playing before a home crowd in Boston against the best players of the National League, he put on quite a show in the 1946 All-Star Game on July 9, with four hits in four at-bats, including a pair of home runs.

The most memorable swat came when Pittsburgh Pirates pitcher Truett "Rip" Sewell threw his famous blooper pitch, a slow, sky-high rainbow that frustrated overanxious hitters. Williams followed the ball patiently and blasted it into the seats.

1946

shifted everyone but the left fielder to the right side of second base—where Williams most often hit the ball. But it didn't stop Williams.

Pesky chipped in with a league-best 208 hits, and asthmatic pitcher David "Boo" Ferriss won 25 games. The Red Sox won the pennant by 12 games.

Things were much tighter in the National League, where the St. Louis Cardinals and Brooklyn Dodgers finished tied at 96 wins, necessitating the first playoff in Major League Baseball history. The Cardinals, who were powered by Stan Musial (.365, 228 hits) and Enos Slaughter (130 RBI), won consecutive games against Brooklyn and claimed their fourth pennant in five years (the first under new manager Eddie Dyer).

The World Series in October was a classic. The two featured hitters fell flat—Musial batted .222, Williams only .200 with one RBI—but the evenly matched teams traded wins and were tied after six games.

St. Louis took a 3–1 lead in game seven, but DiMaggio tied it up with a two-run double off screwball pitcher Harry Breechen, who had come on in relief after winning game six. In the top of the eighth inning, Slaughter faced off against Red Sox reliever Bob Klinger. Slaughter's availability had been in doubt, since he was hit by a pitch on the right elbow in game five. Klinger, because of an illness in his family, was pitching for the first time in 27 days. Slaughter won this confrontation with a single.

After outs by third baseman Whitey Kurowski and catcher Del Rice, outfielder Harry Walker singled to left center-field. Slaughter was running on the pitch and when centerfielder Leon Culbertson came up with the ball, Slaughter kept running…and running.

Pesky caught the outfield throw and turned to face home plate, but hesitated before throwing the ball home. His throw went 10 feet up the first base line, and Slaughter scored the go-ahead run.

"You could almost say it was a dumb play that worked," catcher Joe Garagiola said about Slaughter's sprint. "You know the difference between dumb and smart—the word 'safe.'"

Breechen retired the Red Sox in order in the top of the ninth inning to win his third game of the World Series. The Cardinals were champions.

The College Football End-Around

Football players who had left college to fight in the war regained their eligibility upon return, plus funds for college from the GI Bill—but nothing said they had to play for their old schools. The resulting scramble excited coaches and angered critics across America.

In the October 14 issue of *Time* magazine, American University President Paul F. Douglas said, "Post-war college football has no more relation to education than bullfighting to agriculture. . . . A football player is nothing more than a human slave caught in the biggest black market operation in the history of higher education."

The *Saturday Evening Post* did its own story, referring to "football's black market." The magazine pointed to Short McWilliams, who had started for Army

Head Man *Coach Frank Leahy (in the cap) meets with his new 1946 Notre Dame team.*

before transferring to Mississippi State University. An MSU booster, it was alleged, offered McWilliams $15,000 in cash, a car, a $300-a-week summer job, and a permanent job after graduation. Oklahoma A&M officials charged that its rival, the University of Oklahoma, spent $200,000 to buy its football team, and that individual players were receiving as much as $10,000 to suit up.

For better or worse, the NCAA did nothing at all.

Much Ado About Nothing–Nothing

The University of Notre Dame's football team won the national championship in 1943. But when coach Frank Leahy joined the Navy soon after, the team quickly declined. As teams re-assembled in 1946, the Fighting Irish of Notre Dame stocked up again. Star quarterback Johnny Lujack joined returning starters such as halfback Terry Brennan, transfers like big tackle George Connor (who came from Holy Cross College), and blue-chip freshman recruits such as end Leon Hart.

The result was fearsome. Thirteen Notre Dame players rushed for more than 100 yards, although none had more than Emil Sitko's 346. The defense held all nine of its opponents to six points or less. In one stretch the Fighting Irish shut out four consecutive opponents.

Notre Dame was coached by the quirky Leahy (1908–1973), a perfectionist who constantly exhorted his players to fight for Our Lady—the Virgin Mary, whom he was certain watched over the Catholic college.

1946

As the Fighting Irish churned through its 1946 schedule, it didn't require advanced calculus to pinpoint the big game. Army's Black Knights had won their last 25 games, and had whipped the Fighting Irish 59–0 in 1944 and 48–0 in 1945.

When the nation's top-ranked teams met on November 9, more than 74,000 fans—including Generals Dwight D. Eisenhower and Omar Bradley—filled New York's Yankee Stadium to the bursting point. The game had been sold out for months, and scalpers were getting $200 a ticket. That was a month's pay for many Americans at the time.

Leahy had been in the Navy during those two Army whippings, but that did not lessen his desire for revenge. During the week's practice before the game, Leahy had his men chanting, "59 and 48, this is the year we retaliate."

The action was as furious as most had hoped. But the defenses completely dominated the day. Notre Dame mounted the only sustained drive of the game marching 85 yards to Army's three-yard line. But the Black Knights' defense held there, and Army took over on downs.

As for the Fighting Irish defense Army ended up with great field position after several intercepted passes and fumble recoveries, but could not take advantage. The closest Army got was the Notre Dame 15-yard line. Glenn Davis and Doc Blanchard combined for a paltry 80 yards on 25 carries. Notre Dame's Lujack completed only six of 17 passes for 52 yards. All three players finished among the top four in Heisman voting that year.

In the end, it was one of the most memorable games of the decade. But the scoreboard never changed from 0–0.

Little Big Man

When Ben Hogan (1912–1992) was nine years old, his blacksmith father committed suicide. Hogan began working as a caddy at a Fort Worth, Texas, golf club at the age of 12, and he turned pro at 17.

Hogan, who was forced to grow up in a hurry, burned with an intensity rarely seen on the golf course. He often practiced for eight hours a day, learning to shoot long drives and to use every club in the golf bag with precision.

"I can't explain it, because I'm not a psychologist," his contemporary and fellow golfer, Byron Nelson, said. "But players were genuinely afraid of him, afraid of playing with him. He wasn't ugly to them, but there was something about that cold stare of his."

Hogan, who stood just 5-foot-9, did not really heat up until 1946, when he returned from service in the U.S. Army Air Corps at the age of 34. He won the PGA tournament that year, beginning a streak of nine victories in 16 majors.

Hogan didn't slow down for 15 years. From 1946 through 1960, he never finished out of the top 10 in a major tournament in the United States. In 1953 he became the first golfer to win three of four majors in one year. Only Tiger Woods has matched that feat.

After the standoff with Army, Notre Dame won 21 straight games. The Irish also won the 1946 national championship, the first of three in just four seasons. (The freshmen who entered in 1946 graduated with a sparkling 36–0–2 record.)

Unbowed by any opponent, the Irish could be deterred only by their own administration. School officials, concerned that football was outpacing the importance paid to academics, cut the number of scholarships in half, and the team fell to 4–4–1 in 1950.

Battle of the Military

After its epic scoreless tie with Notre Dame, Army managed to hang on to the nation's number-one ranking. Three weeks later, on November 30, the Black Knights took the field for their last game of the season, against Navy, in front of approximately 100,000 fans at Philadelphia's Municipal Stadium.

Army had arranged to bring its entire cadet corps down from West Point in a 36-car train. But a strike by the United Mine Workers resulted in a coal shortage. The cadets arrived in 50 buses instead.

Navy had won its first game of the 1946 season, then dropped seven straight as injuries struck down its five best backs. The Navy Midshipmen began the Army game as 28-point underdogs, and were down 21–6 at halftime. But Army started to look vulnerable in the second half. Navy marched 78 yards for a third-quarter touchdown and, after stopping the Black Knights on fourth-and-goal, added another score on a pass from Bill Earl to Leon Bramlett at the start of the fourth quarter. Unfortunately, Navy missed all three of its extra points; instead of a 21–21 tie, the Midshipmen trailed 21–18.

After several changes of possession, Navy got the ball with seven and a half minutes remaining. As the clock wound down and the afternoon light grew dim, the team started to drive. On fourth down from the Army 23-yard line, fullback Lynn Chewning broke away for a twisting 20-yard run, leaving Navy at first-and-goal at the three-yard line.

One minute, 23 seconds remained. The crowd surged out of the stands and gathered along the sidelines, with most voices cheering for the Navy underdogs. Chewning ran right, then left, and was stopped twice for no gain. On third down, Navy hesitated and was hit with a delay-of-game penalty, moving the line of scrimmage back to the eight-yard line. Another run gained four yards. The Navy Midshipmen desperately tried to get in position for a field-goal attempt, but the gun sounded, ending the game and their dreams of an upset.

Navy's one consolation: It had knocked Army from its top spot in the polls. After this game, Notre Dame became number one. Army would never again be the college football powerhouse it was in 1944–45.

The Quiet Pioneers

Jackie Robinson was still a year away from integrating Major League Baseball. But meanwhile, with little fanfare, four black men shattered a barrier that had cast a shadow over professional football since 1933. The Los Angeles Rams

1946

signed halfbacks Kenny Washington and Woody Strode—both of whom had played with Jackie Robinson at UCLA—and the AAFC's Cleveland Browns signed guard Bill Willis and fullback Marion Motley (1920–1999).

Washington, hobbled by bad knees, played three seasons in Los Angeles; Strode played only one. But Willis and Motley later made the jump to the NFL, and both ended up in the Pro Football Hall of Fame. Before getting that far, they had to weather the same hatred and racism that would define Robinson's early career.

"We went down to play Miami one time in 1946, and they told Paul that the two black guys had to stay at a different hotel," Browns quarterback Otto Graham recalled. "Paul said, 'Okay, let's all go.' The whole team was going to go, but then the hotel changed its mind and let us stay. That stuff went on all the time."

Jurassic Shaq

Basketball's popularity had grown substantially during the war, because it required few players and little equipment. When the conflict ended, two professional basketball leagues began vying for the public's attention—and money. The National Basketball League (NBL) had quietly operated in the Midwest for several years. It was now challenged by the Basketball Association of America, with teams in Boston, Chicago, Cleveland, Detroit, New York, Philadelphia, Pittsburgh, Providence, St. Louis, Toronto, and Washington, D.C.

Goaded by the competition, the NBL made headlines when the Chicago Gears

Pacific Time

Despite a growing population and a track record of supporting minor-league sports, the West Coast had no professional sports teams at all before the end of World War II. Many had discussed it. Before the 1940 Major League Baseball season, for example, a group of West Coast businessmen put together $5 million to entice a team. The St. Louis Browns and Philadelphia Phillies both said no. The overriding reason was long-distance travel. It had once been almost impossible. Now it was merely expensive.

The migration finally occurred in 1946, and it was the AAFC that spurred it. The new football league placed teams in San Francisco (the 49ers) and Los Angeles (the Dons). It was a public-relations coup.

But the NFL was not to be outdone. Cleveland Rams owner Dan Reeves had been petitioning his league for the right to move to Los Angeles for some time. He claimed to have lost $50,000 in 1945. With a new threat at the gates, owners granted Reeves permission, and 27 days after winning the NFL Championship Game against the Washington Redskins, the Rams moved to Los Angeles in January 1946.

Suddenly, the biggest city in the West had not one, but two professional football teams.

Other Milestones of 1946

✔ Assault, ridden by jockey by Walter Mehrtens, won horse racing's Triple Crown.

✔ Lloyd Mangrum won the U.S. Open golf tournament in June, edging Byron Nelson and Vic Ghezzi by a stroke after all three had tied in the first playoff round.

✔ The New York Yankees became the first baseball team to travel exclusively by air, signing a contract with United Air Lines.

✔ Bert Bell replaced Elmer Layden as the commissioner of the NFL.

✔ After spending three years in the military, the Pittsburgh Steelers' "Bullet" Bill Dudley returned to lead the NFL in rushing (604 yards), interceptions (10), and punt returns (385 yards).

Alice Coachman

✔ Amos Alonzo Stagg completed his final year as a college football coach. He coached a record 57 seasons, the last 14 at University of the Pacific.

✔ Alice Coachman became the first black woman to join the U.S. All-American track and field team.

✔ The Ladies Professional Golf Association (LPGA) was formed.

✔ Hockey legend Gordie Howe (b.1928) played the first of his 32 seasons as a pro, starting out with the Detroit Red Wings.

✔ The automatic pinspotter, which reset knocked-down bowling pins mechanically, made its debut in bowling, which soon became America's top participation sport. Previously, the pins had to be reset by hand.

---

signed George Mikan (see page 82), the All-America center, for $60,000 over five years. It was considered an absurdly generous contract; the Gears were defunct in a year.

He Got His Title

By 1946, Sugar Ray Robinson had just about everything a boxer could ask for: good health, a nearly spotless record, and the respect of the boxing world. About the only thing he lacked was a championship belt.

That finally changed on December 20, when Robinson outboxed Tommy Bell in a 15-round decision to claim the vacant welterweight title. Over the next four years Robinson beat every man he faced, including future welterweight champion Kid Gavilan (twice) and future middleweight champ Bobo Olson.

1947

The Fancy Pants Triumph

The meteoric college basketball team of 1946–47 was College of the Holy Cross. The Crusaders had no gym and played in Boston, where fans cared a lot more about hockey and baseball than they did about hoops. Coached by Doggie Julian, the team had a deft shooter in All-America pick George Kafton, and enough tricky ball handlers to make frustrated opponents label their style "fancy pants." Holy Cross went 24–3, then triumphed 58–47 over University of Oklahoma in the NCAA tournament title game in March.

The most dynamic player on the Crusaders' roster was freshman and future Basketball Hall of Famer Bob Cousy (b.1928). Holy Cross did not win another basketball championship, but the team was a contender every year because of Cousy's behind-the-back dribbling and no-look passes—which made him the NBA's most famous player in the 1950s.

Everything Is Changed

In the winter of 1947, Brooklyn Dodgers president Branch Rickey ordered his AAA team manager to move Jackie Robinson from second base to first. Rickey then had his major league manager, Leo Durocher, tell a few sportswriters that a solid first baseman was all Brooklyn needed to win the pennant.

Rickey's intentions were clear. He was ready to make Robinson the major leagues' first African-American player in 50 years. Immediately, several Dodgers, led by pitcher Hugh Casey, threatened to quit if they had to play with a black man. Rickey said he would accept their resignations, and they backed off.

On April 15, Robinson started for the Dodgers at first base, and forever changed the game of baseball; some would say he also forever changed America.

The near-mutiny on the Dodgers was just the beginning. Playing the Philadelphia Phillies in late April, Robinson was taunted viciously by Ben Chapman, the Phillies' Alabama-born manager. "At no time in my life have I heard racial venom and dugout abuse to match the abuse that Ben sprayed on Robinson that night," sportswriter Harold Parrott noted. "Chapman mentioned...the repulsive sores and diseases he said Robinson's teammates would become infected with if they touched the towels or the combs he used."

Historic Moment *First baseman Jackie Robinson was part of the Dodgers' starting infield on April 15, 1947.*

Robinson kept his emotions hidden, although friends knew he could have a fiery temper. Chapman's behavior only succeeded in galvanizing Robinson's supporters. Fans wrote letters of protest to Commissioner Happy Chandler, and newsman Walter Winchell criticized the Phillies' manager on his popular Sunday-night radio broadcast. Chapman and Robinson soon posed for a photo together, each smiling through clenched teeth.

Then, on May 9, the *New York Herald-Tribune* wrote of an alleged plot by members of the St. Louis Cardinals to strike rather than play against a black man. According to the newspaper, National League president Ford Frick (1894–1978) said anyone who pulled such a stunt would be banned from baseball. Cardinals players categorically denied the report.

Robinson may have been making civil rights history in 1947. But his presence

1947 had another effect, certainly anticipated by Rickey—who never stopped being a businessman. The rookie was generating impressive ticket sales across the league. At Philadelphia and Cincinnati in May, his visits set attendance records.

Robinson's appeal was twofold. Many white fans came to see him out of a sense of novelty. And blacks turned out in huge numbers to pay homage to their instant hero. Thousands of black fans stood to applaud Robinson at every Dodgers' road game. A "Jackie Robinson Special" train ran all the way from Norfolk, Virginia, to Cincinnati for Dodgers–Reds games, loading up fans along the way.

"The noble experiment had less to do with brotherhood than it had to do with business," University of California at Berkeley sociologist Harry Edwards once reflected. "Finally it became clear there was all this Negro talent out there, all these Negro fans."

As African Americans poured into National League stadiums, they changed the dynamic of spectator sports in America. This was the first time some whites and blacks found themselves in a place where they could mingle, and many whites were surprised to discover how much they and the black fans had in common.

Robinson's season certainly had its ugly moments, but it was largely a success. He scored 125 runs and won the first balloting for Rookie of the Year, for both leagues combined. Voters in an annual public-opinion poll named Robinson the second most popular man in America, behind singer Bing Crosby.

In a wider sense, sports had brought the races together in an intimate way that no amount of legislation or court decisions could. As baseball writer Roger Kahn wrote, "By applauding Robinson, a man did not feel that he was taking a stand on school integration or on open housing. But for an instant he had accepted Robinson simply as a hometown ball player. To disregard color, even for an instant, is to step away from old prejudices, the old hatred. That is not a path on which many double back."

Still, Robinson's presence didn't exactly open the floodgates of integration in Major League Baseball. The Dodgers signed several Negro League stars in the next two years, including Roy Campanella and Don Newcombe, and Cleveland's Larry Doby broke the American League color line in 1948. But many teams remained all-white for years.

Instant Hero *Young fans, black and white, clamored for Robinson's autograph at Ebbets Field in Brooklyn. While many fans treated him as a hero, others did not give him such a warm reception.*

Satchel Paige

The Negro Leagues, which had been the only place African-American players could play pro baseball before 1947, had its sluggers, its slick-fielding outfielders, and its fleet base stealers. But none of them drew a crowd like Leroy "Satchel" Paige (1906–1982), the one-of-a-kind pitcher who was part athlete, part entertainer.

Born in a Mobile, Alabama, ghetto, the seventh of 11 children, he picked up his nickname while carrying bags at the train station at the age of seven. He was pitching for the local Mobile Tigers at the age of 18, and by 1930 he was legendary throughout the South.

Paige was at his best while throwing for the Kansas City Monarchs of the Negro American League, leading them to four straight pennants. Even then, he pitched for other teams as needed. His appearances were likened to old-fashioned minstrel shows. He would call in the outfielders, stand alone on the field, and strike out the side, or throw apples instead of baseballs when the light went bad. Here's one description of a game in Newark, Ohio, written by Tristam Potter Coffin:

> "Between innings, Paige sat in a rocking chair and sipped from a black bottle. He used all his eccentric pitches, throwing overhand, sidearm, underhand; showed the batters the hesitation pitch, the two-hump blooper, the fastballs Long Tom and Little Tom."

Paige finally got to play in the newly integrated major leagues in 1948. He won six and lost one for the Cleveland Browns as a 42-year-old, aiding the team's American League title run. He returned to pitch in 103 games for the Browns in 1952–53, although by then he was approaching 50. And he was barnstorming (playing exhibition games)—and still attracting huge crowds—long after that.

Here Comes Cookie

The 1947 World Series in October featured baseball's most popular player, the New York Yankees' Joe DiMaggio, and its man of the hour, the Brooklyn Dodgers' Jackie Robinson. But the wild six-game shootout wound up being dominated by virtual no-names.

The Yankees came out swinging and won the first two games. Game two was notable primarily for the fielding adventures of Dodgers centerfielder Pete Reiser, who fell down chasing one triple, lost two others in confusion, let a pop fly fall in front of him for a double, and misplayed a single. Game three was just as sloppy. After eight pitchers and three hours, five minutes of play (it was the longest World Series game to that time), the Dodgers won 9–8.

The next game was the one that left fans in disbelief. Yankees starter Floyd "Bill" Bevens had a fastball like lightning, but his accuracy was always a question. He had foundered to a 7–13 record in 1947. In game four of the Series, he was at his unpredictable best and worst. After eight innings on a cold afternoon at Ebbets Field, Bevens had surrendered eight walks. He was also three outs away from becoming the first pitcher to throw a no-hitter in a World Series game. The Dodgers had scored once in the fifth inning (on two walks, a bunt, and an infield out), but trailed 2–1 as they came to the plate for their last at-bat in the bottom of the ninth.

1947

Catcher Bruce Edwards drove the ball to the leftfield wall for a long first out. Carl Furillo walked. John "Spider" Jorgensen fouled out. Reiser came up as a pinch hitter, but when pinch runner Al Gionfriddo stole second (on a poor throw from the young Yankees' catcher, Yogi Berra), Yankees manager Bucky Harris ordered Reiser walked intentionally. It was Bevens' 10th walk.

Dodgers manager Burt Shotton—the temporary replacement of Leo Durocher, whom Commissioner Happy Chandler had suspended for consorting with gamblers—then turned to Harry "Cookie" Lavagetto to pinch hit. Lavagetto was a popular veteran who had inspired the chant, "Lookie, lookie, lookie, here comes Cookie." But in 1947 he hit .261 in only 69 at-bats.

With the count no balls and one strike, Lavagetto drilled the ball past right-fielder Tommy Henrich. Gionfriddo scored, and so did pinch runner Eddie Miksis. Bevens lost the game, the no-hitter, and the Series lead on one pitch.

There was more excitement in the Series. After the Yankees won another one, game six wound up being even longer, at three hours, 19 minutes. With two Yankees on base and the Dodgers leading 8–5 in the sixth inning, DiMaggio hit the ball straight at the 415-foot sign in left-centerfield at Yankee Stadium. It was just over the wall—and then it was in the glove of Gionfriddo, who somehow managed to cover a huge distance and make a sweet backhanded catch while leaning into the bullpen. The Yankees lost.

But the Yanks won game seven behind relief pitcher Joe Page, who shut down the Dodgers over the final five innings, and Henrich, who delivered his third game-winning hit of the Series.

The strangest twist to this wacky Series was that the three top performers—Bevens, Lavagetto, and Gionfriddo—were all playing their last professional games.

The Mad Magicians

The University of Notre Dame won the official NCAA football championship in 1947. But by the time the season was over, many were lauding coach Herbert "Fritz" Crisler's Mad Magicians of Ann Arbor (the University of Michigan Wolverines), so named because of their fabulous ball-handling skills.

Like many postwar teams, the Wolverines were a varied lot. The standouts included tackle Alvin Wistert (not to be confused with his NFL brother, Albert Wistert), a 31-year-old former Marine; tailback Bob Chappuis, who had been shot down over Italy during World War II and listed as missing in action for three months; and Chalmers "Bump" Elliott, the speedy wingback.

Crisler, who had turned down both the AAFC (which wanted him as its commissioner) and the University of California at Berkeley after the 1946 season, was a pioneer in the two-platoon system of substitution (in which players played only defense or offense, rather than both). He ran a type of offense called the single wing, with Chappuis in the primary passing position.

After going 9–0 in the regular season (only two games were even close), Michigan accepted an invitation to play University of Southern California in the Rose Bowl on January 1, 1948. Crisler invited his old coach at the University of Chicago, the revered Amos Alonzo Stagg, to address his team before the game. "Score the first touchdown and keep scoring," Stagg told them. And that's what the Wolverines did, destroying the eighth-ranked USC Trojans 49–0.

The Associated Press had already crowned Notre Dame college football champions, based on polling conducted three weeks earlier. Now it mailed a special ballot, asking each member newspaper which team it preferred, Michigan or Notre Dame. The tally was 226 for the Wolverines and 119 for the Irish, with 12 calling it a tie. Despite the change of heart, the Associated Press ruled that its original vote would be the ranking of record. Still, the Mad Magicians had scored a moral victory. They would get more than that when they won the championship outright in 1948.

Chicago Dreaming

The Chicago Bears had captured six NFL titles since 1925. In that same 22-year period, the Bears' South Side neighbors, the Cardinals, had gone dry. The Cardinals' fortunes began to change in 1946, though, when fullback Pat Harder and right halfback Elmer Angsman joined quarterback Paul Christman in the backfield.

The final piece of the puzzle was Charley Trippi, the Heisman Trophy runner-up from the University of Georgia. And he didn't come cheap. Cardinals owner Charles Bidwill found himself in a bidding war with Dan Topping, who owned the AAFC's New York Yankees, and wound up signing Trippi to a princely four-year, $100,000 contract.

Trippi took his spot at left halfback in the Cardinals' T-formation, and collectively the four men became known as the "Dream Backfield." Finally the South Siders had something to cheer about as their Cardinals won the Western Division and hosted the Philadelphia Eagles in the NFL Championship Game at Chicago's Comiskey Park on December 28.

The Dream Backfield turned out to be a pure nightmare for the Eagles. Trippi scored on a 44-yard run and a 75-yard punt return, breaking five tackles. Angsman ran for a pair of 70-yard touchdowns, and the Cardinals prevailed 28–21.

The Cardinals have relocated twice since, first to St. Louis and then Arizona, and are still waiting for their next title.

A New Spin

At Yale University, one of the oldest student traditions was to take the sloped pie tins of a local bakery—the Frisbie Pie Company of Bridgeport, Connecticut—and toss them back and forth. In 1947, two enterprising Californians took the game to a higher level.

Fred Morrison and Warren Francioni made a flying disk of plastic and called it the Frisbee. The toy caught on quickly, and before long the name was patented by the Wham-O Manufacturing Company of San Gabriel, California. A half-century later, Frisbee-catching dogs are be a staple of football halftime entertainment.

1947

Still the Best . . . Maybe

One thing World War II hadn't been able to change was that Joe Louis was still the heavyweight champion. He had started to slip, but no one else was good enough to take away his belt.

On December 5, Louis faced Jersey Joe Walcott (1914–1994), a veteran boxer who had been fighting for years with mixed results. Bookmakers put Walcott's odds at 15–to–1. But he stunned the New York crowd, knocking down the champion in the first and fourth rounds and outboxing him for much of the fight.

Louis exited the ring after the last round, apparently figuring he had lost. But two of three judges gave the decision to the champion, who then apologized to Walcott.

The rematch came on June 25, 1948, and again Walcott tormented Louis with his quick moves. This time, there was no judges' decision. Louis awoke to batter his foe in the 10th round, then knock him out in the 11th round. But these victories, far from being sweet, only served to show how far Louis had fallen since his glory days.

The Birth of Speed

Bill France (1909–1992) spent the war as foreman at the Daytona Beach Boat Works, which manufactured submarine chasers. When the conflict ended, he returned to his first love—building and racing cars, primarily on the sand.

Big Bill (as the 6-foot-5 France was called) loved racing, but he saw that an average driver in an expensive car could usually beat a good driver in a lesser car. His dream was to create an organization in which all the cars operated within the same guidelines—"stock cars," so to speak.

On December 14, France assembled 25 men at the Streamline Hotel in Daytona Beach, Florida. He talked about codified rules and a points system that would crown a national champion. He stressed the importance of clean, brightly painted cars. "Nothing stands still in the world," Big Bill said. "Things get better or worse, bigger or smaller."

It was mechanic Red Vogt who came up with the name for their group that everyone liked: the National Association for Stock Car Auto Racing—NASCAR.

On February 15, 1948, six days before incorporating NASCAR, France held the first race on Daytona Beach. The winner was Red Byron. He was driving what was called a "modified" car. NASCAR had to wait until 1949 for true stock cars; the Detroit auto plants were still backed up with new-car orders, having ceased commercial production during the war.

To this day, control of NASCAR remains in the France family.

Guile Over Power

It was a white day-after-Christmas in New York, where a blizzard dropped 25 inches of snow and snarled traffic. That might have spelled bad news for the opening match of the 1947–48 pro tennis tour. Instead, 15,114 people found their way to Madison Square Garden.

The match pitted the reigning tour champion, Bobby Riggs (1918–1995), against the graduating amateur champ,

Other Milestones of 1947

✔ The Philadelphia Warriors won the first championship of the Basketball Association of America, four games to one over the Chicago Stags, in March.

✔ Fans begin to choose the starting lineups for the Major League Baseball All-Star Game with a mail-in ballot.

✔ The University of California at Berkeley beat Yale University in baseball's first College World Series in June. Yale's first baseman was future President George Herbert Bush.

✔ The first Little League World Series was held in Williamsport, Pennsylvania, in August. A local team, Maynard Little League, won the tournament.

✔ Althea Gibson won the first of 10 consecutive American Tennis Association season titles. The ATA

Warriors star Joe Fulks

put on a series of amateur tennis tournaments for African-American players.

✔ The annual NHL All-Star Game was played for the first time on October 13, before the start of the season. In 1962, it moved to its current spot in midseason.

✔ Former New York Giants outfielder Danny Gardella sued Major League Baseball for $350,000, saying the major leagues' reserve clause is a violation of national antitrust laws. The reserve clause bound players to the team that first signed them. Gardella eventually settled for $60,000, and the reserve clause was not challenged successfully until the 1970s.

✔ Ted Williams won his second baseball Triple Crown.

Jack Kramer (b.1921). It was a study in contrasts. At 5-foot-8, Riggs had a soft serve and rarely put much power on his shots. But he tracked down the ball in every corner of the court and had a vast array of shots, from lobs to chops to dinks, all kissed with unpredictable spin. He drove foes crazy.

Kramer symbolized "the big game" that was coming into vogue. Instead of playing soft shots for long rallies, Kramer aimed to overpower his opponents with powerful serves and volleys. He was tall, and he could serve like a cannon. He played like he didn't have time for long rallies.

As the match got under way, Kramer was shocked to see Riggs charging the net, a tactic Riggs rarely used. Meanwhile, Riggs' spinning serves were keeping Kramer off-balance. Riggs took the first set 6–2, and the second 10–8. The crowd roared.

But Kramer sent hard shots down the line repeatedly in the third set, and finished with consecutive aces (a serve that the opponent cannot return) to take the set 6–4. The battle continued, until Riggs' slicing returns finally wore Kramer down. Riggs won the fourth set 6–4, and the match along with it.

Kramer recovered to win the pro tour that season, and became the first tennis player known primarily for his achievements as a professional.

1948

Let the Games Return

There was no better indication that the world had returned to some semblance of normalcy after World War II than the Olympic flag flying over St. Moritz, Switzerland, in February. The Winter Olympics were back after 12 years and two cancellations (Sapporo, Japan, in 1940 and Cortina d'Ampezzo, Italy, in 1944). The ski-resort town had been practically untouched by the war, and 28 nations sent 706 athletes to the Games.

The United States made a decent showing in the Winter Olympics, ranking fourth overall with 19 medals and tying for third with three golds.

Skier Gretchen Fraser of Vancouver, Washington, clocked the fastest time in the first run of the women's slalom skiing event. But as she prepared to lead off the second round, the telephone timing system that connected the top of the hill with the bottom stopped working. Fraser waited 17 minutes in the chute, but turned in a strong time anyway and won the gold. She also took silver in the alpine combined event.

The U.S. four-man bobsled team—a burly group from Lake Placid, New York, who averaged 224 1/2 pounds—also overcame technical difficulties before finishing first. Competition was halted in the middle of the second round when a water pipe burst and flooded the bobsled run.

For John Heaton, the hurdle wasn't technology but time. He won consecutive silver medals in the skeleton (a type of sledding performed headfirst and facedown) 20 years apart. He was 19 years old the first time, 39 years old in 1948.

Resolute as a Button

Dick Button (b.1929) had been a rolypoly child, 5-foot-2 and 162 pounds at the age of 12. Dismissed by a figure skating coach, he worked hard to lose weight and hone his skills on the ice. By 1946, Button won the U.S. men's figure skating championship. In 1948, now 18 years old and a freshman at Harvard University, he was the country's best hope to win a gold medal in figure skating—something no American had ever done.

As the leader heading into the final round, Button was faced with a dilemma. He had completed a double axel jump for the first time only three weeks earlier. Should he attempt the flashy move

nowy Star *American skier Gretchen Fraser was a gold medalist at the first Olympic Games after World War II.*

low, or be cautious? Button went for the gusto and nailed the double. Eight of nine judges gave him their highest score; only one, the Swiss judge, gave the highest score to Swiss skater Hans Gerschwiler. Button went home with the gold medal.

A week after the Olympics, Button won the world championship in Davos, Switzerland. He then launched a tour to show off his athletic style, which was characterized as uniquely American. One of the stops was Prague, Czechoslovakia, which had just fallen to Soviet-backed Communist soldiers. As Button entered the rink, he was greeted with a hail of oranges. "I thought this was the Czech

Tale of the Red Tape

The Olympics are supposed to represent an ideal of human competition, where athletes rise above the petty issues of the day. Alas, politics intrude here as they do elsewhere. When the 1948 Winter Olympics began, two U.S. hockey teams arrived ready to compete. One was sanctioned by the American Hockey Association (AHA), the other by the American Olympic Committee (AOC), whose president, Avery Brundage (1887–1975), accused the AHA of commercialism.

The Swiss Olympic Committee ruled that the AOC team could take part in the opening ceremony, and the AHA team would then play all the games. The International Olympic Committee (IOC) countered by nullifying the entire tournament. The Americans (the AHA team) won by some amazing scores, beating Poland 23–4 and Italy 31–1. In the end, though, the IOC announced it would sanction the tournament only if the AHA team didn't appear in the standings. To this day, it does not.

version of an anti-American raspberry, and I threw the first orange off the rink," he said. "However, when others were thrown, I picked one up and noticed the paper in which it was wrapped had some encouraging words written on it: GOOD LUCK, U.S.A. Another said, COME ON, BUTTON!" In the new Cold War world, things were not always what they seemed.

Major Deals

Hockey was tough business in the 1940s, but it didn't intimidate Conn Smythe (1895–1980), general manager of the Toronto Maple Leafs. Smythe spent 14 months in a German POW camp during World War I, and was wounded while commanding Canada's 30th Antiaircraft Battery in World War II. "World War III,"

Tim Crothers wrote in the book *Greatest Teams*, "was any game Smythe's Maple Leafs played against the Detroit Red Wings."

Over the decade of the 1940s, the man they called the "Little Major" assembled an indomitable crew. Centers Syl Apps and Ted "Teeder" Kennedy, and chubby goalie Turk Broda had been there for Toronto's championship in 1942. After the war, Smythe added the "Gold Dust Twins"—defensemen Jimmy Thomson and Gus Mortson—and winger Howie Meeker, who nearly had his leg shattered by a grenade during the war.

The Maple Leafs were known for their clutch-and-grab tactics and frequent brawls. But their style triumphed over artistry in the 1947 Stanley Cup finals when they upset the Montreal Canadiens in six games.

Before the start of the 1947–48 season, Smythe shocked Leafs' fans by trading five of his champions to the Chicago Blackhawks for touted center Max Bentley. Smythe also found another gem that year when he signed 19-year-old defenseman "Bashing" Billy Barilko, who soon was slamming opposing players against the boards around the league.

In the finals in April, Toronto swept past Detroit in four games. They swept the Red Wings again in 1949, becoming the first NHL team to win three straight Stanley Cups.

A Privilege to Ride

Ask veteran horse racing fans to name the greatest horse of all time and many of them will say Citation.

ertainly, few horses have had a year to
match the bay colt's run in 1948, when he
won 19 of his 20 races and finished second
in the other. Citation not only was fast
and determined, but he also had great
endurance over the course of a race. He
didn't just win the Triple Crown that year,
he ran away with it.

Before the first race of the Crown,
the Kentucky Derby, the talk among racing fans was that Coaltown was an even
stronger horse than Citation. Certainly,
Coaltown was a faster sprinter. The question was, could he keep up his speed over
a mile and a quarter? Breeders entered
only four other horses, none of them contenders, against the swift duo.

The sun shone as the Derby got
under way on May 1, but rain had mud-
died the track. Coaltown broke strong
from the gate, with Citation falling in behind. By the time they reached the far
turn, Coaltown was seven lengths ahead.
Finally, jockey Eddie Arcaro on Citation
made his move. As they came out of the
turn and galloped down the stretch, Citation cut the lead to two lengths, then one,
then pulled even. Coaltown matched the
pace for a few strides, then fell back, and
Citation won by three and a half lengths.

Arcaro had his fourth Derby victory—
a record—and Citation was on his way to
greatness. He entered the Preakness
Stakes as a 1–10 sure thing and led from
start to finish, winning by five and a half
lengths. "It is a crime to take the money for
riding such a horse," Arcaro said after
that race. "It is a privilege."

Citation completed his sweep by taking the Belmont Stakes on June 11 by
eight lengths. When the colt came to the

The Best Ever? *Citation, ridden by legendary jockey Eddie Arcaro,
charges after Coaltown on the way to winning the 1948 Kentucky
Derby, the first leg of Citation's Triple Crown.*

post for the Pimlico Special that autumn,
he couldn't find a single challenger. So
he breezed around the track solo and
picked up $10,000.

Citation developed an osselet, or hot
spot, on his left foreankle and did not
compete in 1949, although a thoroughbred's fourth year is often its best. Still, he
returned to race successfully, and became
the first horse to claim more than $1 mil-
lion in prize money.

Citation was the fourth Triple Crown
winner of the 1940s. But no horse would
win another until Secretariat in 1973.

London Calling

It was a pleasant feeling to have the
Summer Olympics in London, which
had survived heavy bombing just a few
years earlier. But as the Games got under

1948

way in July, the hostilities of World War II were too raw—and the global landscape too uncertain—to ignore.

Olympic organizers did not invite Germany, Italy, and Japan, the vanquished Axis powers. And Joseph Stalin's Soviet Union, which quickly changed from America's ally to its chief rival, refused to participate. In June, Soviet troops cut off all surface access to the western sector of the newly divided German city of Berlin. When the Games began a month later, British and American airplanes were flying in food, medical supplies, and fuel to needy Berliners.

Still, a record 59 nations sent athletes to the unseasonably cold and wet British capital to participate in the Games. Without the Soviets there, the United States flattened the competition, winning more gold medals (38) than the next three nations combined (Sweden, France, and Hungary, with a total of 36).

Some of the more notable American winners included:

- Alice Coachman (b.1923) squeaked past Britain's Dorothy Tyler on a technicality in the women's high jump and became the first black woman to win an Olympic gold medal.

- Harrison "Bones" Dillard (b.1923), who, as a boy, received his first pair of running shoes from the great Jesse Owens and went on to win an unprecedented 82 consecutive races. In London Dillard looked like a sure thing in the 110-meter hurdles, but hit three hurdles and stopped running. Fortunately, he had narrowly qualified for the 100 meters as well. The competition

was fierce, including record-holders : both the 100 yards and 100 meter After one false start, Dillard sprint to the lead and broke the tape in virtual tie with fellow American No wood "Barney" Ewell, who danced an hugged his opponents in appare victory. After reviewing a photo, how ever, judges gave Dillard the gold.

- Air Force sergeant Mal Whitfie pulled away in the 800-meter race f the gold. Between 1948 and 195 Whitfield won 66 of 69 races at th distance.

- Wilbur Thompson, F. James Delan and James Fuchs outdistanced the re of the world by more than three fe while sweeping the medals in th shotput.

- The U.S. basketball team survived 59–57 threat from Argentina in an ear round (not to mention one comic moment when a Chinese player dri bled between the legs of Bob Kurlan the seven-foot American center, a scored a basket) to win the gold eas ly. The final score against silver med ist France was 65–21.

- Bill Smith took up swimming to bui strength after contracting typho fever at age six. He set an Olymp record in the 400-meter freestyle.

- The U.S. women's 4-by-100-met freestyle relay swimming team can from behind to take the gold ov Denmark, after a spectacular anch swim by Ann Curtis (b.1926). Her tir of 1:04.4 would have set the wor record if it had not come in the rel

Amateur Champion

By the time Bob Mathias turned 11, he was high-jumping five feet and long-jumping 15. Then he suffered a bout of acute anemia (low iron in his blood), followed in rapid succession by chicken pox, measles, and whooping cough. His father, a Tulare, California, physician who had played football at the University of Oklahoma, helped Mathias regain his strength with vitamins and a healthy diet.

At 17, Mathias entered his first decathlon and scored the highest point total by an American in seven years. Over the next four years, he never lost a decathlon.

After his amazing performance in the 1948 Olympics, Mathias went to Stanford University, where he played football and helped lead the Stanford Indians to the 1952 Rose Bowl. Later that year he claimed gold in the decathlon at the Summer Olympics in Helsinki, Finland, becoming the sport's first two-time Olympic champion.

He never got a shot at a third gold medal. The Amateur Athletic Union declared him a professional after he was paid to star in a biographical movie, *The Bob Mathias Story*.

Mathias proved to be a tireless fighter for amateur athletes. He lobbied for passage of the Amateur Sports Act of 1978—sometimes called the athlete's "Bill of Rights"—and helped guide the establishment of the U.S. Olympic Training Center in Colorado Springs.

- Vicki Draves grew up in San Francisco, the child of a Filipino father and an English mother. She became the first female diver to win two gold medals (springboard and platform) in one Olympics.

- Light-heavyweight lifter Stanley Stanczyk was given credit for a world-record snatch of 132.5 kilograms, only to startle the referee by confessing that his knee had scraped the floor—a disqualification for that lift. Fortunately, Stanczyk's muscles were as well-developed as his sportsmanship. He won the competition by 37.5 kilograms, the widest margin in Olympic weightlifting history. The silver medalist, American Harold Sakata, later gained fame for his portrayal of Oddjob in the James Bond movie *Goldfinger*.

Boy Wonder

Late in Bob Mathias' senior year at Tulare (California) High School, his track coach suggested he consider the decathlon, a track and field sport that combines 10 events. Mathias (b.1930) had never done a pole vault or a long jump, thrown a shotput or a javelin, or run a distance race. But he was confident enough to enter an Olympic regional meet three weeks after the decision, and he stunned observers by winning. A couple weeks after that, he claimed first place at the U.S. national meet in Bloomfield, New Jersey, securing a spot on the 1948 Olympic team.

At age 17, Mathias was the youngest athlete in the history of the U.S. track and field team. The veteran decathletes who gathered in London to compete against him were distinctly unimpressed.

1948

The first day of competition (five of 10 events were scheduled), August 5, was dark and wet. After decent performances in the 100 meters and long jump, Mathias surprised himself with a long shotput. But the novice exited the ring from the front, something he now learned was forbidden. This throw was disqualified, and his next throw wasn't as good.

He ran a swift 400 meters, but faltered in the high jump, twice missing at 5-foot-9. Huddled under a blanket, Mathias made a desperate decision. He abandoned the Western roll technique prevalent at the time (in which the athlete throws one leg over the bar and then "rolls" over with the chest facing the ground) and sprinted straight at the bar, then leaped awkwardly. He cleared the barrier, went on to jump 6-foot-1 1/4, and finished in third place.

The second day's weather was even more dismal, with rain and heavy fog delaying the decathlon until the afternoon. After the 100-meter hurdles and the discus, Mathias had claimed the lead.

By the time officials set up the pole vault, it was 9 p.m. The vaulters had to run down a darkened path toward a bar illuminated with flashlights. Mathias, weakened from effort and lack of food (he hadn't eaten since devouring a box lunch), passed up the preliminary jumps. It was a risky strategy, because he'd be penalized if he failed at 10 feet and would almost certainly lose any hope for the gold medal. But he cleared the bar at 11 feet, 5 3/4 inches.

Mathias won the javelin throw and finished the 1,500 meters in 5:11, quick enough to win the decathlon. He was the youngest person to win an Olympic gold medal in track and field.

No Rain in October

The Boston Braves had a pair of dominant pitchers in 1948. Johnny Sain won 24 games, pitched 315 innings, and recorded 28 complete games. Warren Spahn (b.1921) won 15 games and threw 257 innings (actually an off year for the man who eventually had more wins—363—than any other lefthander in history). Braves' fans knew the recipe for success, and it became a familiar refrain: "Spahn and Sain and pray for rain."

In the World Series in October, Boston met the Cleveland Indians, who had a fine pitching staff of their own, paced by Bob Feller and Bob Lemon. Cleveland's pitchers were just too much for the Braves, who scored one run or less in each of the first four games, before breaking out with 11 runs in game five.

Gene Bearden, a Navy veteran who had aluminum plates in his head and knees because of war wounds, pitched a five-hit shutout for the Indians in game three, then retired the last four Braves in the decisive sixth game. It was Cleveland's first World Series championship since 1920.

Final Innings

Jackie Robinson's arrival in Major League Baseball in 1947 (see page 66) signaled a bittersweet era for African-American fans. On one hand, black players now got to compete with the best players in the world, make solid money, and get their names in mainstream newspapers. On the other hand, the change spelled doom for the Negro Leagues that had flourished for decades. The point was hammered home in 1948, when the Negro National League ceased operations after the season.

Nobody would have traded the new opportunities for the old way of life, but there was an aura about the Negro Leagues that couldn't be recaptured. The season usually began in February. Teams barnstormed all over the South, often picking up players along the way. "Rarely were we in the same city two days in a row," said Roy Campanella, who starred for the Baltimore Elite Giants before gaining fame with the Brooklyn Dodgers.

The exhausting tours could include three games in a day. The last, called the twilight game, ended when the hitters could no longer see the ball. Barred from white hotels and restaurants, the players and coaches often slept in private homes, or even on team buses.

The Negro Leagues reached their apex during the war. Some 2 million fans attended games in 1942, and the popular East-West All-Star Game attracted 51,000 spectators in Chicago that year. But when Robinson broke the major league color barrier, the end was inevitable. The Negro American League fielded only four teams in 1953, and struggled mightily before giving up for good in 1960.

Ice Festival

The Philadelphia Eagles and Chicago Cardinals had been so undermanned in 1943 and 1944 that they took turns combining with Pittsburgh to form one team (see page 38). Just a few years later, in 1948, they squared off for the NFL title on December 19. But before going head to head, players from both

Athletic Artistry

Pro football was becoming more colorful in the 1940s—in terms of action, at least. When it came to headgear, the NFL was bland and colorless.

That changed in the spring of 1948, when Fred Gehrke of the Los Angeles Rams' showed his drawings of a yellow ram's horn on a blue background to head coach Bob Snyder.

Gehrke was an accomplished artist as well as a halfback (he had been a technical illustrator for Northrop Aircraft during the war), and the coach loved his drawings. So did Rams owner Dan Reeves. Gehrke painted a helmet each night over the next sum-

mer—75 total, all by hand—lining them up in his garage. The Rams paid him $1 per helmet—just enough to cover the cost of paint—and he touched them up every week throughout the 1948 season.

Gehrke got a break the following year, when the Riddell sporting goods company introduced plastic helmets to the NFL, replacing the old leather version. Now the paint could be applied by machine, baking on the design under a layer of translucent plastic.

The Baltimore Colts soon painted a blue horseshoe on their white helmets, and within a decade most of the teams in the league followed suit.

1948

teams joined forces to pull the snow-covered tarpaulin off the field at Shibe Park in Philadelphia. A blizzard was raging.

Within 30 minutes, the field was blanketed with snow again. Officials marked the sidelines with ropes tied to stakes, while the stadium lights cast eerie shadows on the great piles of snow. Amazingly, 28,864 people braved the blizzard to watch the game in the stadium.

The first time the Eagles had the ball, quarterback Tommy Thompson hit end Jack Ferrante with a 65-yard touchdown pass. For a moment, no one noticed the white penalty flag on the white ground; Ferrante had been offside (he moved before the play began). After that, the game settled into a brutal series of inside runs. Chicago quarterback Paul Christman was

taken out with an injury. Philadelphia's Steve Van Buren, who rushed for 98 yards, seemed to be the only player able to handle the footing. "It was sloppy but not slippery," the star halfback later remembered. "I could run okay, I just couldn't see. It was snowing so hard, I couldn't even see the Cardinals' safety, Marshall Goldberg."

Late in the third quarter, Chicago quarterback Ray Mallouf and halfback Elmer Angsman fumbled a handoff, and Philadelphia's Frank Kilroy recovered the ball at the Cardinals' 17-yard line. Four plays later, Van Buren scored from five yards out, giving his team a memorable 7–0 victory.

When the Lakers Were Really Near a Lake

To say George Mikan was the NBA's first superstar wouldn't be doing him justice. The big man actually predated the now-established league. Playing for the Minneapolis Lakers in 1947–48, he teamed with forward Jim Pollard to dominate the National Basketball League's (NBL's) Western Division. After averaging 21.3 points per game in the regular season, Mikan shot an average of 27.5 in the final series against the Rochester Royals, leading the Lakers to a three-games-to-one victory.

Before the 1948-49 season, the Lakers—along with the Royals, the Fort Wayne Zollner Pistons and the Indianapolis Kautskys—defected to the Basketball Association of America (BAA). Mikan averaged 28.3 points in a season when only two other players in the league broke 20. On February 22, 1949, Mikan

Nice Day to Be Inside *Parka-clad Philadelphia Eagles players shiver on the sidelines while watching their teammates in the snow-covered 1948 NFL Championship Game, won by the Eagles 7-0.*

Other Milestones of 1948

✔ The Harlem Globetrotters defeated the Minneapolis Lakers 61–59 in an exhibition game on February 19, before 17,853, the largest crowd ever to see a professional basketball game in Chicago. It was the Globetrotters' sixth game in six nights.

✔ The University of Michigan captured the first NCAA ice hockey championship, beating Dartmouth College in the final round at Colorado Springs in March.

✔ Bowman resumed producing trading cards of sports figures, having curtailed the business during World War II. Topps followed suit in 1951.

Larry Doby

✔ Larry Doby batted .301 in 439 at-bats for the Cleveland Indians. Doby had broken baseball's color line in the American League when he debuted for the Indians on July 5, 1947.

✔ The National Boxing Association announced a new safety program, including a mandatory eight count after knockdowns, and the use of heavily padded eight-ounce gloves.

✔ Forty American rodeo performers—male and female—were escorted to the French border after they were involved in a brawl with spectators and police in Geneva, Switzerland.

---

set a pro scoring record when he poured in 48 points in a 101–74 victory over the New York Knicks.

The big man broke his wrist during a game against the Washington Capitols (coached by Red Auerbach) in the 1949 finals, but scored 22 points with a cast on his hand in game five. The Lakers claimed the BAA title a game later.

The Lakers then built a 29-home-game winning streak in 1950, only to see it end when the Pistons stalled play all game long and won 19–18.

No one ever called Mikan fast, but he knew how to get position in the paint (the area under the basket), and his shooting touch was excellent. (He could hit the hook shot reliably with either hand.) Mikan's greatest asset was his size—6-foot-10, which was supersized when compared to most centers at the time. He probably looked even bigger than he was—he wore number 99 and played on a court at the Minneapolis Auditorium that was slightly smaller than regulation.

In January 1950, a poll of sportswriters named Mikan the greatest basketball player of the half-century. His playing career was sweet but short. He retired at age 29 to become a lawyer, and later became the first commissioner of the American Basketball Association.

1949

Can't Keep a Great Golfer Down

One of the most closely followed sports stories of the year took place not on a field or a court, but on a foggy highway in Texas. On February 2, golfer Ben Hogan and his wife were driving from California to their home in Texas when a bus suddenly appeared on the road ahead, bearing straight for them. The Hogans' car hit the bus head-on.

Valerie Hogan was fine. But Ben was rushed to a hospital in El Paso, about 100 miles away, where it was reported that he had a double fracture of the pelvis, broken collarbone, fractured rib, broken ankle, and severe internal injuries.

At first no one knew whether he would live. Then there was no guarantee he'd walk again. But Hogan slowly showed signs of improvement, and two weeks after the accident, doctors operated to treat his internal injuries.

Immediately after the operation, the gritty golfer started his rehabilitation program. He began by squeezing a rubber ball to strengthen his fingers, then progressed to stomach exercises designed to mend his abdominal muscles. It wasn't long before he was jogging several miles a day.

Late in 1949, Hogan filed an entry form for the Los Angeles Open, to be held in January 1950. Fans applauded his resolve but expected him to make a token appearance. Instead, Hogan played four strong rounds, resting on a chair between shots. He eventually finished second to Sam Snead, losing in a playoff, but proving he was back in the game after only 11 months.

Wildcats Strike

From 1946 through 1954, the University of Kentucky was the king of college basketball. The Kentucky Wildcats won the NIT title in 1946, fell to the University of Utah in the NIT final in 1947, and claimed the NCAA crown by topping Baylor University in 1948. Even the 1948 U.S. Olympic team was dominated by Kentucky's "Fabulous Five."

Kentucky was back in the hunt in 1949. Fueled by players such as center Alex Groza, guard Ralph Beard, and forward Wallace Jones, the Wildcats went 29-1 in the regular season and entered the NCAA tournament as the nation's top-

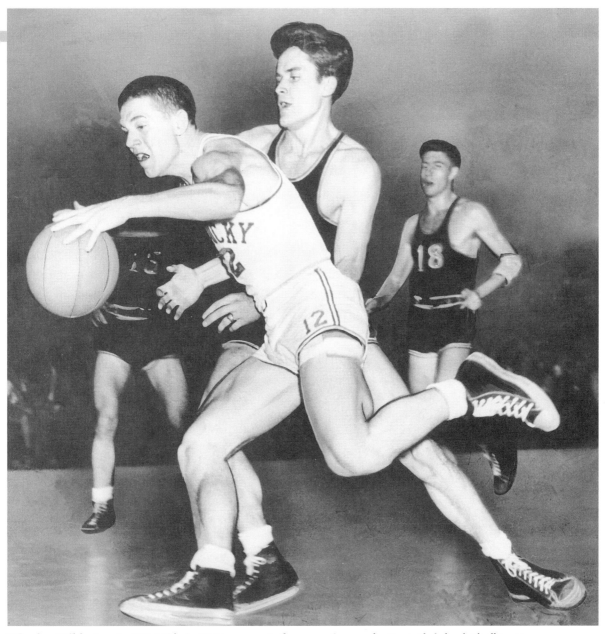

Winning Wildcats *An NCAA title in 1949 was part of an amazing run by Kentucky's basketball team.*

ranked team in the first Associated Press college basketball poll. On March 26, the Wildcats defeated Oklahoma State University 46–36 in the final of the NCAA tournament in Seattle, repeating as champions. The 6-foot-7, 220-pound Groza, labeled a "scoring machine" in the sports pages, rang up 25 points in the final (more than twice as many as any other player), and was the tournament MVP.

Our Old Kentucky Coach

The University of Kentucky has won more games, built a higher winning percentage, and made more tournament appearances than any other team in college basketball history. The man who established the foundation—and, indeed, won nearly half of those games—was Adolph Rupp (1901–1977), known as "the man in the brown suit." He coached the Wildcats from 1931 (when he was 30 years old) to 1972 (when he was 71). Along the way, he led Kentucky to four championships in the NCAA tournament and one in the NIT. He also was among the first coaches to develop the fast break.

Rupp ruled his program with an iron fist. He allowed no sloppy attire, card playing, or towel stealing, saying he had no intention of "packing around a bunch of tramps, gamblers, and thieves."

Kentucky's shining run of success was dimmed, though, when the team got caught up in the gambling scandal of the early 1950s.

Disaster Averted

The 1949 NIT championship in March pitted the University of San Francisco against Loyola University of Chicago. The USF Dons were a strong team that had gone 21–5 during the regular season. The Loyola Ramblers upset Bradley University to reach the finals.

The final score of the title game was USF 48, Loyola 47—but it hides a footnote. Dons center Don Lofgran accidentally tapped in a basket for Loyola, a shot that loomed as a potential disaster as the game went back and forth. Fortunately for Lofgran, his team won anyway. Of course, he had something to do with that, too. The center scored 20 points for USF and was named tournament MVP.

Birth of the NBA

It was clear that America wanted professional basketball in the late 1940s. It was equally clear that the country could not support two separate leagues. So after the 1948–49 season, the Basketball Association of America and the National Basketball League merged into a single entity, the 17-team National Basketball Association (NBA). Its original teams included the Waterloo Hawks, the Sheboygan Redskins, and the Indianapolis Olympians.

Seventeen teams proved to be far too many. The NBA cut down to 10 teams by the 1950–51 season, and down to eight by 1954–55. From that point on, it experienced nothing but gradual growth.

Red's Run

By 1949, race drivers had enough new cars at their disposal that Big Bill Elliott and the folks at NASCAR could call their series Strictly Stock. This is the year many people regard as the true birth of stock car racing.

The first Strictly Stock race was at Charlotte (North Carolina) Speedway—a 3/4-mile dirt oval at the county fairgrounds—on June 19. The winner, Jim Roper, would never be a big name in NASCAR. But the second race, at Daytona, Florida, was captured by Robert "Red" Byron. He had spent two years in military hospitals as doctors attended to his mangled left leg, wounded when his Air Corps bomber was shot down.

Driving a new Oldsmobile with a specially extended clutch pedal, Byron captured the 1949 championship after an eight-race series. He won a second race and collected a whopping total of $5,800 in prize money. His tiny hometown—Talladega, Alabama—would one day become an important center of auto racing.

The Strictly Stock Series evolved into the Grand National Division, and later into the Winston Cup Series. It became the Nextel Cup Series in 2004.

Net Profits

In the 1940s, tennis remained largely an amateur sport. Professional tours came and went, their membership changing constantly. Many players chose to remain amateurs.

Jack Kramer wasn't the first tennis player to turn pro, but when he organized an extensive national pro circuit in the fall of 1947, it forever changed the structure of the sport. His players included well-known personalities such as Bobby Riggs, Pancho Segura, and Don Budge, and their matches drew big crowds.

The notion got a little bigger on September 20, when star Pancho Gonzalez (1928–1995) signed a one-year pro contract with Riggs, who had become a promoter. The contract guaranteed Gonzalez $60,000 the first year. Kramer and Gonzalez then combined on a tour that began at Madison Square Garden in New York on October 25.

Boomer Sooners

Throughout the 1940s, college football was dominated by teams from the Midwest (Notre Dame, Ohio State,

Minnesota) and the military academies (especially Army). But a new power began to emerge in 1948, when Bud Wilkinson's University of Oklahoma Sooners capped a thrilling season with a 14–6 victory over third-ranked University of North Carolina in the Sugar Bowl. The Sooners earned top-20 rankings in 1946 and 1947, too, but now they were a true force to be reckoned with.

Oklahoma was in full bloom in 1949. Wilkinson (1916–1994) was a soft-spoken and professorial young coach with a master's degree in English and experience as a hangar-deck officer on an aircraft carrier during World War II. He coached at Oklahoma for 17 seasons and won three national championships in the 1950s, but many observers feel the 1949 team was Wilkinson's best.

The Sooners were hot from the first play of the first game of the season, when the sensational George Thomas fielded the opening kickoff against Boston College and ran it back 95 yards for a touchdown. They won 46–0 and never looked back. By the end of the regular season, Oklahoma was 10–0 and ranked number two in the country, behind Notre Dame.

It was too late for the official rankings (which were settled before the bowls then), but the Sooners' 35–0 drubbing of Louisiana State in the Sugar Bowl on January 1, 1950, made them a popular choice as America's best college team.

Heck on Wheels

Leo Seltzer figured he'd have a box-office smash when he developed roller derby, a sport that involved roller-

1949

skating around a circular track and pretending to slam into the opponents. It was a dud for years, however, until Seltzer had a brilliant idea. In 1947 he televised a game in Chicago, and it was a sensation. When people saw roller derby on television, they rushed to see live matches.

By 1949, roller derby (male and female) was being staged in arenas across America, drawing several million paying fans. "The Derby's disruptive effect on the household is virtually absolute," *New York Times* media columnist Jack Gould wrote. "Never before has roller-skating meant so much."

Round and Round They Went *The rough sport of roller derby, played on roller skates on wooden indoor ovals, enjoyed enormous popularity in the late 1940s and early 1950s.*

The first World Series of the National Roller Derby filled Madison Square Garden for a week in September, with crowds as large as 13,000. Those numbers grew to 19,000 by 1951. In the mid-1950s, however, television executives flooded the airwaves with games. Roller derby became all too commonplace, and attendance gradually declined.

Peace Time

The competition between the NFL and the AAFC was great for football players, who saw their salaries skyrocket. (Before the war, players were getting an average of $150 per game; by 1949 the average minimum salary was $5,000 per year.) It generally piqued fan interest, too. But the four-year league war had devastated the two leagues financially.

Groups representing the rival organizations met in Philadelphia in December of 1948, but talks broke down. So the AAFC forged ahead with the 1949 season, reducing its schedule from 14 games to 12 and merging two teams, Brooklyn and New York. Money was so tight in Chicago that players from the Hornets (a new ownership group had changed the team name from the Rockets) and the visiting Cleveland Browns had to clear the field of snow before their game.

Cleveland dominated the AAFC again. During the four years of league play, the Browns went 47–4–3 and won all four championship games. By 1949, none of the other franchises could come close to Paul Brown's team.

The NFL, for its part, also struggled under the strain of competition. On

Other Milestones of 1949

✔ Bill Lewis, the first black man selected as an All-American in football (during the 1892–93 season), died on January 1 at the age of 80.

✔ Baseball's New York Yankees hired Casey Stengel as manager, ushering in a new winning era for the team.

✔ Marcenia Lyle Alberga was the first woman to play a full season in a men's semipro baseball league.

✔ In July, Major League Baseball owners mandated warning tracks in all stadiums. These strips of dirt still ring the playing surface. Players chasing fly balls can keep their eyes on the ball,

Casey Stengel

knowing that the feel of dirt under their feet will alert them that they are nearing a wall or other barrier.

✔ The NFL permanently permitted free substitution, allowing any player to be substituted after each play. Previously, players removed from a game could not return in the same quarter.

✔ George Blanda joined football's Chicago Bears as a rookie. He didn't retire until 1975, when he was the oldest active player at age 48.

✔ College basketball coaches were given permission to talk to their players during time outs.

December 9, the two leagues announced a merger agreement.

Under the terms of the pact, the NFL absorbed the Browns, the San Francisco 49ers, and the Baltimore Colts (who had joined the AAFC in 1947 and finished 1–11 in 1949), beginning in 1950. Players from the other four AAFC teams would be dispersed in a draft.

The new body was called the National-American Football League. That lasted about two months, after which it reverted back to the good old NFL.

Down and Dirty

A week after the NFL-AAFC announcement, the Philadelphia Eagles met the Los Angeles Rams in the NFL Championship Game. The Eagles had won the title the year before, thanks in part to the snowstorm that blanketed Philadelphia and favored their physical style of play (see page 81). The 1949 game, by contrast, was to be played in Los Angeles, where Rams quarterback Bob Waterfield and end Tom Fears were used to endless sunshine and big passing plays.

But the skies opened up on December 17, the day before the game, and three inches of rain fell by kickoff. It was the first time the Rams had played a home game in the rain since they moved west in 1946, and the field was a sloppy mess.

Steve Van Buren again starred for Philadelphia, splashing for 196 rushing yards. End Pete Pihos caught a 31-yard touchdown pass from Tommy Thompson, Len Skladany scored after blocking Waterfield's punt, and the Eagles won the championship 14–0.

RESOURCES

1940s Events and Personalities

America Prepares for War
By Wallace B. Black and Jean F. Blashfield (New York: Crestwood House, 1991)
This book explores the United States' military presence in World War II, even before America officially became part of the conflict following the attack on Pearl Harbor on December 7, 1941.

Babe Didrikson Zaharias: The Making of a Champion
By Russell Freedman (New York: Clarion Books, 1999)
The most remarkable female athlete of her time—and perhaps of any time—Babe Didrikson Zaharias excelled at just about any sport she tried.

Breakthrough to the Big League: the Story of Jackie Robinson
By Jackie Robinson and Alfred Duckett (North Bellmore, New York: Marshall Cavendish Corp., 1991)
Originally written in 1965, this is the autobiography of the baseball pioneer.

Franklin D. Roosevelt: the Four-Term President
By Michael Schuman (Springfield, New Jersey: Enslow Publishing, 1996)
This book chronicles the life of the man who guided the United States through one of the most important eras in its history.

American Sports History

The Encyclopedia of North American Sports History
Edited by Ralph Hickok (New York: Facts On File, 1992)
This title includes articles on the origins of all the major sports as well as capsule biographies of key figures.

Encyclopedia of Women and Sport in America
Edited by Carol Oglesby et al. (Phoenix: Oryx Press, 1998)
A large overview of not only key female personalities on and off the playing field, but a look at issues surrounding women and sports.

Encyclopedia of World Sport
Edited by David Levinson and Karen Christensen (New York: Oxford University Press, 1999)
This wide-ranging book contains short articles on an enormous variety of sports, personalities, events, and issues, most of which have some connection to American sports history. This is a great starting point for additional research.

ESPN SportsCentury
Edited by Michael McCambridge (New York: Hyperion, 1999)
Created to commemorate the 20th century in sports, this book features essays by well-known sportswriters as well as commentary by popular ESPN broadcasters. Each decade's chapter features an in-depth story about the key event of that time period.

Facts and Dates of American Sports

By Gordon Carruth and Eugene Ehrlich (New York: Harper & Row, 1988)
Very detailed look at sports history, focusing on when events occurred. Large list of birth and death dates for major figures.

The Sporting News Chronicle of 20th Century Sports

By Ron Smith (New York: BDD/Mallard Press, 1992)
A good single-volume history of key sports events. They are presented as if written right after the event, thus giving the text a "you are there" feel.

Sports of the Times

By David Fischer and William Taafe (New York: Times Books, 2003)
A unique format tracks the top sports events on each day of the calendar year. Find out the biggest event for every day from January 1 to December 31.

Total Baseball

Edited by John Thorn, Pete Palmer, and Michael Gershman. (New York: Total Sports, 2004, eighth edition)
The indispensable bible of baseball, it contains the career records of every Major Leaguer. Essays in the front of the book cover baseball history, team history, overviews of baseball in other countries, and articles about the role of women and minorities in the game.

Total Football

Edited by Bob Carroll, John Thorn, Craig Neft, and Michael Gershman (New York: HarperCollins, 2000)
The complete and official record of every player who has played in the NFL. The huge book also contains essays on a wide variety of topics relating to pro football.

Sports History Web Sites

Baseball Library

www.baseballlibrary.com
This is a great reference site for biographies of Major League Baseball players — from the 1940s or from any other decade..

ESPN.com

www.sports.espn.go.com
The Web site run by the national cable sports channel contains numerous history sections within each sport. This one for baseball is the largest and includes constantly updated statistics on baseball.

Hickok Sports

www.hickoksports.com
Not the most beautiful site and devoid of pictures, but filled with a wealth of information on sports at all levels. It is run by Ralph Hickok, an experienced sportswriter, and is regularly updated with the latest winners.

Official League Web Sites

www.nfl.com
www.nba.com
www.mlb.com
www.nhl.com
Each of the major sports leagues has history sections on their official Web sites.

The Sporting News "Vault"

www.sportingnews.com/archives
More than 100 years old, The St. Louis-based Sporting News *is the nation's oldest sports weekly. In the history section of its Web site, it has gathered hundreds of articles on sports events, championships, stars, and more. It also includes audio clips of interviews with top names in sports from yesterday and today.*

INDEX